The Hamburg Model – exemplary integration of youth into vocational education

Elina Priedulena

Published by
Baltic Sea Academy e.V.
Dr. Max A. Hogeforster
Blankeneser Landstrasse 7,
22587 Hamburg, Germany

Editorial Correspondence: editor@baltic-sea-academy.eu
©2015 Baltic Sea Academy e.V.; all rights reserved.

Printed by:
BoD-Books on Demand, Norderstedt, Germany
ISBN 9783738630060

The project "Hamburg Model" has been co-financed by the European Commission (Lifelong Learning Programme). This publication reflects the views only of the author, and the Commission cannot be held responsible for any use which may be made of the information contained therein.

The project "Future perspective: Annual Professional Qualification (Hamburg Model)" was carried out from October 2013 to September 2015 by the Hanse-Parlament e.V. as Lead Partner and eight partners from Germany, Latvia, Lithuania, Norway, Poland and Hungary.

Project management: Dr. Jürgen Hogeforster and Elina Priedulena

We thank the the following authors for the book contributions:

Renata Černeckienė

Habil. Dr. Prof. Romualdas Ginevičius

Dr. Jürgen Hogeforster

Dr. Michał Igielski

Philipp Jarke

László Kajos

István Mosóczi

Dora Szegő

Dr. Monika Zajkowska

Content

1. Introduction 7

2. The dual system of vocational training in Germany 10

2.1. Division of responsibilities 12

2.2. School education background of the trainees 15

2.3. Training centers in the dual vocational training system 17

2.3.1 Training center - Enterprise 17

2.3.2 Training center – Vocational school 18

2.3.3 Inter-company training centers 19

2.4. Faculty staff in the dual educational system 20

2.5. Financing of the dual system 21

2.6. Educational reasons for companies 25

2.7. Strong points of the dual vocational training system 29

2.8. Weak points of the German vocational training system 32

2.9. Trends and consequences for vocational education 33

2.10. Theses on consequences for Baltic Sea Region 36

3. Integration of slower learner into vocational education and training system 40

4. Hamburg Model 45

4.1. Framework concept 45

4.2. Hamburg Model with professional qualification 48

4.3. Professional qualification 50

4.4. Graduation, graduation certificate, leaving 57

4.5. Continuation and completion of training 58

4.6. Hamburg Model with Professional Qualification (PQ) in the profession: Metalworkers . 62

5. Implementation of the Hamburg Model in Lithuania and Hungary 67

5.1. Implementation of the Hamburg Model in Lithuania 67

5.2. Implementation of the Hamburg Model in Hungary 76

6. Evaluation of the piloting of the Hamburg Model in Lithuania and Hungary 82

6.1. Evaluation results of the training in Lithuania 82

6.2. Evaluation results of the training in Hungary 91

7. Recommendations for implementation of the Hamburg Model 123

8. Outlook 129

8.1. Feasibility studies for three Sub regions of the Province of Pomerania by Hanseatic Academy of Management in Slupsk 129

8.1.1. Introduction 129

8.1.2. Characteristics of sub regions from pose of the metropolis Tricity in the Pomeranian province 132

8.1.2.1. Słupski Sub region 133

8.1.2.2. Południowy Sub region 134

8.1.2.3. Nadwiślański Sub region 136

8.1.3. System of the vocational education - the current state and crucial problems 137

8.1.3.1. Vocational education in Poland 137

8.1.3.2. Problems of the vocational education in the Pomeranian province 140

8.1.3.3. Meaning of the dual system of the vocational training 141

8.1.3.4. German model of the dual vocational training 146

8.1.3.5. Situation of graduates of schools carrying the vocational training out in the school system on the Pomeranian labour market 149

8.1.3.6. Barriers and hampering of the implementing the dual system of the vocational training in the Pomeranian province 152

8.1.3.7. The dual system of the vocational training as the response to needs of the labour market in the Pomeranian province 156

8.1.3.8. Declared action assumed by authorities for the development of the vocational training in the Pomeranian province 159

8.1.3.9. Summary and Recommendations 159

8.2. Vocational education and training in Baltic Sea Region – Problems to be addressed 164

8.3. Survey on the dual system of the vocational education in Baltic Sea Region 168

8.4. Work-Based Learning around the Mare Balticum – Results of the Working groups 176

8.5. Strategic Programme of the Baltic Sea Academy - Promotion of Dual Systems of Vocational Education 184

8.5.1. Action Programme "Hamburg Model" 187

8.5.2. Action Programme "Dual Vocational Education and Dual Studies" 189

Other Publications by the Baltic Sea Academy 194

Members of the Hanse Parlament 198

Members of the Baltic Sea Academy 200

1. Introduction

In some of the European Union states up to 15% of school leavers cannot begin a professional education, have to stay in long queues or do not obtain professional education at all. Up to 30 % of young people who begin vocational training abandon it completely or change the profession during the vocational training. The professional education has significantly lost its appeal in most of the EU countries. Especially in the new EU countries (e.g. Poland, Lithuania, Latvia) with predominantly school based vocational training the participation has even dropped to an alarmingly low level.

On the other site Small and Medium-sized Enterprises (SMEs) complain about lack of qualifications of vocational school graduates and the increasing lack of skilled professionals. However, in the contest for young qualified workers SMEs threaten to be the losers. Due to the lack of qualified staff, innovation in SMEs is already much lower than it might or should actually be. The shortage of young entrepreneurs, managers and professionals limits most the growth of SMEs. Improvement of qualification, accompanied by elimination of shortage of skilled labour is the most important supportive task and the central key to sustainable promotion of innovation, competitiveness and growth of SMEs in the Baltic Sea Region.

The implementation and the strengthening of the dual vocational education and training make crucial contributions to the problem-solving described above. Hence, for five years in Hamburg a model, so called Hamburg Model, of one-year professional qualification within the dual system for young people was successfully introduced. This is a proven method to integrate young people into the professional education, who would otherwise not get this chance. Moreover, the Hamburg Model makes the choice of the profession more certain, decreases drop-out rates and increases the chances on the labour market significantly. The one-year professional qualification can be acknowledged as the first year of the professional training. While or after one year of learning the students can continue with the regular dual professional education.

After the further development and adaptation of the model to the country-specific conditions it is implemented in two countries with predominantly school-based vocational training: Vilnius and Budapest.

In connection with the transfer and implementation of the Hamburg Model the German dual vocational training system and experiences should be broadly transferred and thus initiations of Work-based Learning supported.

The broad networks of the Hanse-Parlament with about 50 Chambers of Crafts, Industry and Commerce and the Baltic Sea Academy with 17 universities from countries of the BSR act as permanent developers, promoters and consultants of the Hamburg Model and the dual system in the whole Baltic Sea Region. Hence, high sustainability and broad effect are achieved.

These all activities are carried out within the Lifelong Learning Programme, Leonardo da Vinci, Innovation Transfer project "Future perspective: Annual Professional Qualification - Hamburg Model" (DE/13/LLP-LdV/TOI/147613) from 2013-2015.

The main objectives of the project are:

a) Integration of young people with poor chances on the education market into the regular vocational education and training by implementing the Hamburg Model, thus reduction of drop-outs, improvement of qualifications as well as chances on the labour market and reduction of youth unemployment is achieved.

b) Transfer of the German dual vocational training system and support of implementation.

c) Transfer of all results in all the Baltic Sea Region countries and ensuring high sustainability.

Eight partners from six countries are involved in the project:

- PP 0: Hanse-Parlament, Germany, Lead Partner and coordinator of the project activities
- PP 1: Baltic Sea Academy, Germany, elaboration of analyses, PR work, transfer activities
- PP 2: Hamburg Institute for Vocational Education, Germany, core partner, developer and implementer of the Hamburg Model in Hamburg, consultation tasks for implementations in the project
- PP 3: Nordic Crafts Forum, Norway, developer of the feasibility studies about the introduction of the Hamburg Model and dual vocational education system in Norway, experience exchange
- PP 4: Latvian Chamber of Crafts, Latvia, developer of the feasibility studies about the introduction of the Hamburg Model and dual vocational education system in Latvia, experience exchange
- PP 5: Public Institution Vilnius Builder Trainings Centre, Lithuania, implementing partner of the Hamburg Model in Lithuania
- PP 6: Kontiki Vocational Training, Hungary, implementing partner of the Hamburg Model in Hungary
- PP 7: Hanseatic Academy of Management in Slupsk, Poland, developer of the feasibility studies about the introduction of the Hamburg Model and dual vocational education system in Poland, experience exchange

For six months of the project the representative from Poland was the Craft Chamber of Łódź that was involved as project partner with the partner number 7. The Craft Chamber of Łódź had the task to implement the Hamburg Model in Łódź. Once it turned out that the implementation is not possible due to law regulations in the region, the partner asked to leave the project. As the new Polish partner the Hanseatic Academy of Management in Slupsk joined the project to prepare feasibility study of Hamburg Model implementation in Poland (see the results in the chapter 8.1.).

The Transfer Partners are:

- Members of the Hanse-Parlament and
- Members of the Baltic Sea Academy

2. The dual system of vocational training in Germany[1]

The vocational training plays a prominent role in the German educational system. Almost 60 % of each year's students choose professional education. Up to 70 % of them again fall into the dual system while the remaining part of the students completes a full-time school-based education at a vocational school. The system is called dual because the training is performed in two learning places: at an enterprise and at the vocational school. At the moment in Germany the training is possible in 349 acknowledged qualified professions for the duration between 2 and 3,5 years.

The central law for the vocational training in Germany is the Vocational Training Act (BBiG). Other important laws are: the Crafts Code (HwO), the Ordinance on Trainer Aptitude, the Young Persons Employment Act, the Industrial Constitution

---

[1] Jürgen Hogeforster, Lucyna Döding, *The educational systems in the Baltic Sea Region with special consideration of the dual system in Germany*, in: *Job Market Innovations – testing and implementation of new methods of the promotion the employment in the niching, perishing and little popular occupations*, Hamburg 2012; graphics updated and translated from German to English by Elina Priedulena.

Act, the Law for the Advancement of Further Training and the Distance Learning Protection Act.

The legal basis for the enactment of educational regulations are §25 of BBiG or §25 of HwO. There it states that the Federal Ministry of Economics and Technology in consultation with the Federal Ministry of Education and Research officially recognize qualified jobs and can issue educational regulations for this purpose. The educational regulations are prepared at the Federal Institute for Vocational Education and Training (BIBB) by intensive involvement of representatives of the employers and employees.

For the job-related teaching at vocational schools the Permanent Conference of the Ministers of Education and Cultural Affairs of the Federal States (KMK) issues framework plans which are aligned with the educational regulations of the federation. The curricula for the general teaching at the vocational school are developed principally by separate states because culture and education in Germany are subject to the sovereignty of the federal states.

The legal basis for the educational relationship between the enterprise and the apprentice is established by the training contract which must be concluded in writing before the beginning of the training. The following is regulated in the training contract, incl.:

- type, structure and especially the goal of the training
- beginning and duration of the training
- training measures
- duration of the regular daily time of training
- duration of the probation period
- payment method and amount of trainee allowance
- duration of the leave

- preconditions for termination

The training contract must be submitted to the competent authority – in Germany these are corresponding competent chambers – and there it must be registered in the "List of vocational training relationships" if the training suitability of the enterprise is verified.

2.1. Division of responsibilities

The responsibilities in the dual system in Germany are divided as follows.

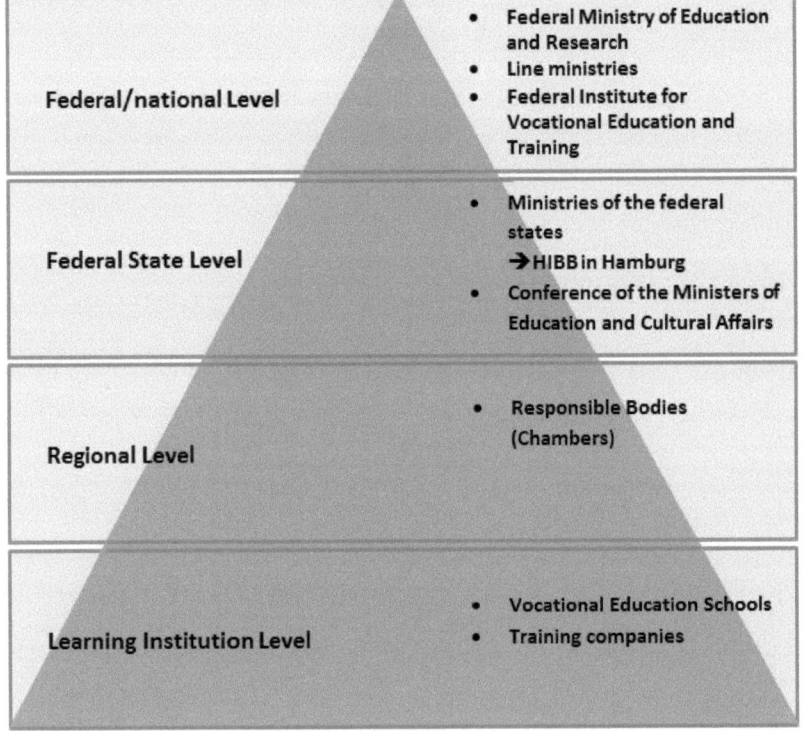

Source: own diagram

1) Framework of the federal law

All the parties involved in the dual education (federation, states and economy) act within the legal framework determined by the Vocational Training Act (BBiG). In addition further labor law provisions of various branches of law are also obligatory for the professional education and further training. So legal provisions and legal principles which are valid for the labour contracts are also valid for this training contract provided that special regulations are not stipulated in the BBiG.

2) Federal Government

The Federal Government is responsible for the contents of the qualified jobs acknowledged by it, provided that the training does not take place at schools. Through the obligatory acknowledgement of qualified jobs in the whole Federation the threshold figures elaborated together with the economies and the states are implemented and at the same time it is ensured that the training for the acknowledged qualified profession may be performed only according to the training regulations issued by the Federal Government.

3) Lands

The lands are fully and solely responsible for the school system. In the dual education it means, that according to the agreement of the states between each other and with other parties involved in the dual education – in respect of the corresponding qualified profession each state shall issue a curriculum for its training at the vocational school. Besides it, states perform legal supervision of the chambers.

4) Economy (employer and unions)

Suggestions for the development or revision of training regulations provided by the economy are taken up by the Federal Government only when they were elaborated in consensus of employers and unions. Independently from the Federal Government the tariff partners stipulate further regulations for the vocational training on the basis of their tariff autonomy especially the amount of training remunerations. In some labour contracts in addition thereto other agreements are stipulated, for example, related to the temporary further employment of apprentices after the training.

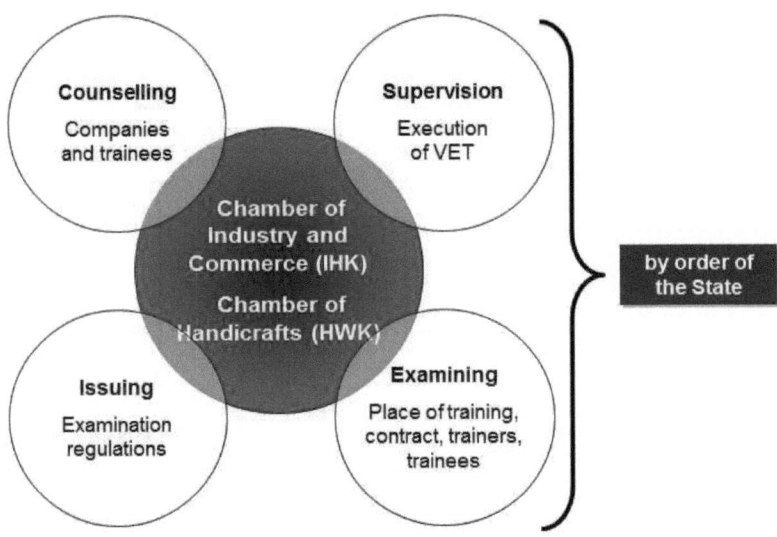

Source: Graphic by R. Damm, Hamburg Institute for Vocational Education (HIBB); presentation during the Kick-Off Workshop of the project "Hamburg Model" in Vilnius, 12.11.2013, http://www.vet-bsr.eu/documents/

5) The chambers

The chambers as self-governing bodies of economy – within the framework of the dual training were assigned public tasks. They include the consulting and the supervision in respect of separate training relationships. Training consultants of the chambers check the training suitability of enterprises and trainers and also consult enterprises and the trainees. They accept training contracts, check and register them. The chambers organize the whole examination procedure by determining the terms and appointing examination commissions, which conduct the examinations. In addition thereto the chambers issue examination and graduation certificates. Examination commissions consist of representatives of employers, employees and vocational schools. Regarding important issues of vocational training the chamber shall hear the vocational training commission, which is to be established and which shall consist in equal proportions of representatives of enterprises, of employees and also of vocational schools in an advisory capacity.

2.2. School education background of the trainees

The statutory requirement for compulsory schooling in Germany begins as a rule at the age of 6 and lasts (depending on the Federal State) 9-10 years. After four years of elementary school the students make a decision about the secondary school within the general three-tier school system:

- the gymnasium, which demanding curriculum is oriented at the acquisition of the general entitlement to study at universities
- the middle school (Realschule), which curriculum leads to obtaining the middle school certificate which certifies broad general educational and vocational preparation qualifications, and
- the secondary modern school (Hauptschule) which is customized for students with practical skills or interests and leads to the secondary school leaving certificate (e.g. introduces to the world of labour).

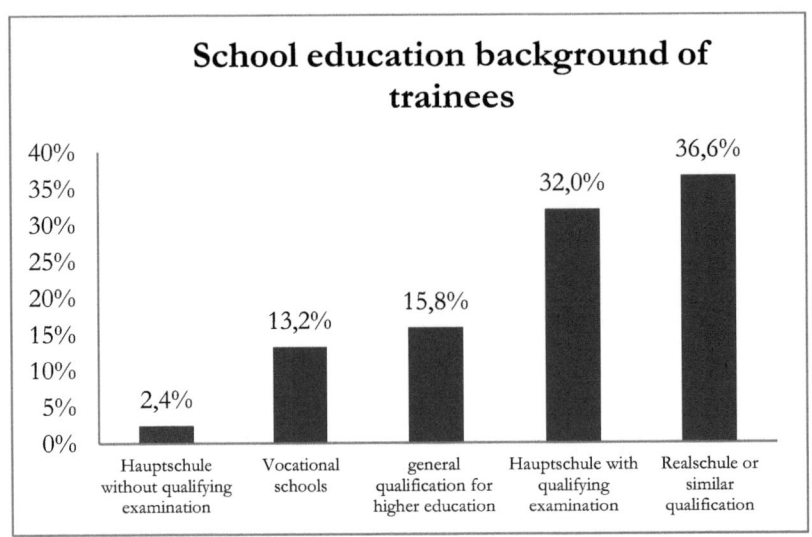

Source: Bundesministerium für Bildung und Forschung (BMBF), Referat für Öffentlichkeitsarbeit (ed.), *Berufsbildung sichtbar gemacht. Grundelemente des dualen Systems*, Bonn 2003, http://www.bmbf.de/pub/berufsausbildung_sichtbar_gemacht.pdf (July 2015); own translation

Different paths often meet up each other in the professional education. Unlike full-time vocational schools, which require a middle school graduation certificate, in the dual system there are no admission requirements for the admission to the education; basically, it remains open for everybody. In practice 36,6 % of the training beginners possess a middle school graduation certificate, 32 % have secondary modern school graduation certificate and 15.8 % have general entitlement to study at universities while 2,4 % have no school graduation certificates. In addition 13.2 % of trainees have completed the vocational school basic education year (BGJ), the vocational preparation year (BVJ) or one-year vocational schools.

The education in the dual system is organized content-wise, so that it can be mastered by young people with at least secondary modern school graduation certificates. To compensate possible level differences on the basis of different educational background the Vocational Training Act or the Crafts Code envisages the reduction and also the extension of the period of training. Thereby it shall counteract the excessive or the insufficient demands in respect of the trainees.

2.3. Training centers in the dual vocational training system
2.3.1 Training center - Enterprise

Trainees usually spend 3-4 days a week in a company providing vocational training, where they are trained in practice on the basis of the training plan according to the provisions of the training regulations prepared with regard to the corresponding profession. The training regulations regulate e.g. the duration of training, describe the job and determine the requirements to examinations.

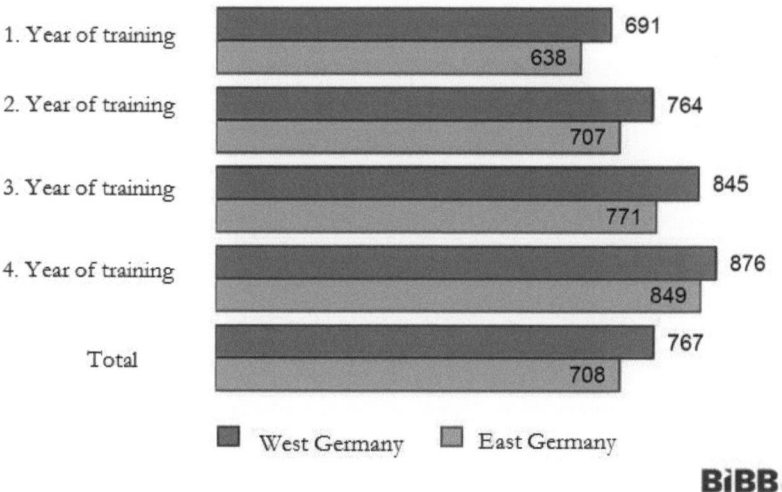

Source: Ursula Beicht, *Tarifliche Ausbildungsvergütungen 2013 erneut stark gestiegen,* Bundesinstitut für Berufsbildung 06.01.2014, http://www.bibb.de/dokumente/pdf/a21_dav_internet-fachbeitrag_azubiverguetungen-2013.pdf (July 2015); own tranlation

The characteristic feature of education is the acquisition of the required professional experience connected with the transfer of knowledge and skills. It guarantees that the training is performed under the same conditions, under which the studied profession will be exercised later. Only at the enterprise the trainee learns, on one hand, how to cope with the changing requirements of the professional practice and, on the other hand, he discovers the various social relations existing in the world of work. Additionally, promoted are independence and the sense of responsibility, because the trainee can demonstrate the obtained knowledge and skills through specific working tasks and in the real working conditions of the working, experiencing the success of his efforts.

During the training the trainee receives remuneration, which increases each year and amounts at the average to one-third of the starting salary of a qualified worker. In 2009/2010 the average monthly educational remuneration (gross) in the first year amounted to 532,97 €, in the second year it was 590,39 € and in the third educational year it amounted to 648,22 €.

2.3.2 Training center – Vocational school

The practical education is supplemented with the theoretical course at vocational schools where students study about 12 hours a week. The teaching takes place on specific days during the week or in blocks.

In vocational schools one-third of the lessons consist of the cross-occupational learning and two-thirds consist of the work-related subjects according to the framework curriculum, which is prepared for separate professions by the Conference of the Ministers of Education and Cultural Affairs for the work-related branch and by lands individually for the cross-occupational learning section. The cross-occupational branch includes, for example, contents of such subjects as Social Studies, Economics,

German, Foreign Language, Religion and Sports. It is closely connected to the work-related contents, but addresses it in a different manner.

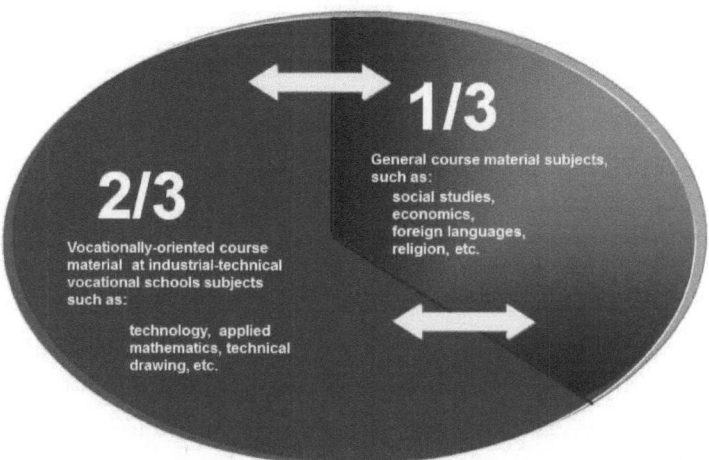

Source: Graphic by Reinhard Damm, Hamburg Institute for Vocational Education (HIBB); presentation during the Kick-Off Workshop of the project "Hamburg Model" in Vilnius, 12.11.2013; http://www.vet-bsr.eu/documents/

2.3.3 Inter-company training centers

It is not always possible for small and medium-sized enterprises to provide complete vocational training in a recognized profession within their own enterprise. In order to facilitate or to enable the provision of vocational training for these enterprises intercompany training centers are available. Besides, not all enterprises possess all the new technologies. Therefore, intercompany training centers offer courses related to new technologies as well as other educational events, which supplement the professional education at small and medium-sized enterprises. These training activities in craft professions last as a rule four to six weeks, in the construction industry - 26 weeks. Number, contents, amount, duration etc. of these supplementary training activities are determined in each case by separate chambers according to the regional conditions with legally binding effect for the corresponding chamber region.

The intercompany schooling activities are a part of the in-company vocational training (of the company educational center). The interplant training centers are usually financed by the chambers or alternatively by the employers' associations.

2.4. Faculty staff in the dual educational system

At vocational schools one can distinguish among two categories of faculty, on one hand, faculty for the purpose of theoretical teaching at vocational schools (vocational school teachers) and, on the other hand, specialist practice faculty (specialist teachers). Vocational school teachers need a university or an equivalent degree and a specialized didactic education. Specialist teachers do not need high school degrees, as a rule they have a respective professional background as a master or specialist (industry) or assistant (crafts). The continuing education for teachers is obligatory and takes place in the form of seminars at state institutions for the continuing education of teachers.

The requirements set for the company trainers are regulated by the Vocational Training Act and in the Ordinance on Trainer Aptitude. According to it trainers must have passed the final examination under the specialty corresponding to the qualified job and possess working pedagogic knowledge. The obligatory trainer aptitude examination was temporarily suspended in August 2003 in order to stimulate the companies to offer more training places; on August 1, 2009 it was introduced again. For company trainers there are no legal requirements for further training.

2.5. Financing of the dual system

Federation, lands and communities as well as the Federal Labor Office spend about 92 bn. € on education which is about 4.1 % of the gross domestic product. Approximately 7.2 bn. € or 7.9 % of them go to the professional education in the dual system[2].

The financing of the dual vocational training is performed according to the division of responsibilities: the enterprises perform the financing of the company part and the Federal States or the local public authorities finance the schooling part of education.

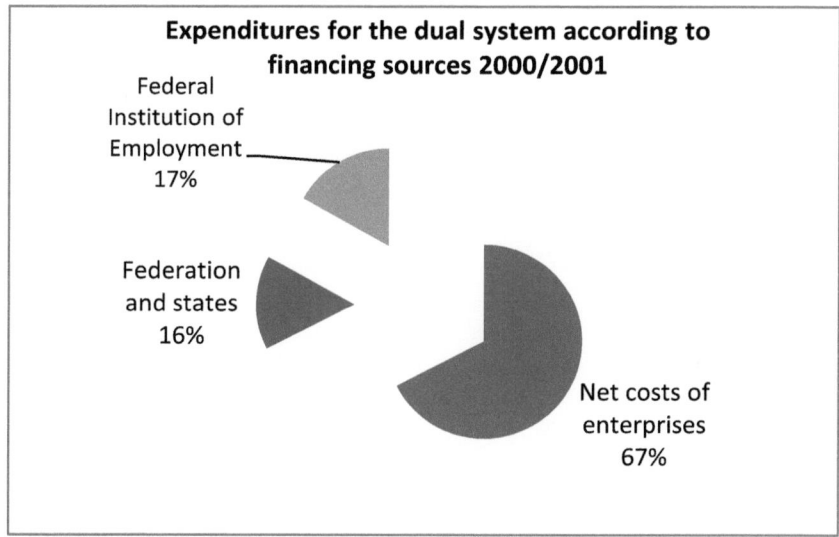

Source: Baumann 2004

---

[2] Thomas Baumann, *Ausgaben für die duale Ausbildung in Deutschland. Methodische Aspekte der Berechnung*, in Wirtschaft und Statistik: Wiesbaden 2004, 888 – 892, https://www.destatis.de/DE/Publikationen/WirtschaftStatistik/BildungForschungKultur/AusgabendualeBildung.pdf?__blob=publicationFile (July 2014).

The diagram shows that the total expenses for the dual vocational training in the year 2000 amounted to about 21.8 bn. €. About two-thirds of expenses for the vocational training at the amount of 14.7 bn. Euro (net costs, including trainee remuneration, minus production profit) were borne by the enterprises while the Federal States spent 3.4 bn. Euro on vocational schools. Further 3.7 bn. Euro were incurred by the Federal Labor Office[3].

In financing of the dual education the companies are given an extremely important role. In 2000 the Federal Institute for Vocational Education and Training has performed the collection of educational costs from the enterprises. According to that the gross expenditures of a crafts company for the education in the dual system in the year 2000 amounted to 14.395 Euro per each trainee. If one takes into account the productive output created at the enterprise by the trainee at the amount of 6.780 Euro the net burden of the employers amounted to 7.615 Euro[4].

---

[3] Ibid., p. 891
[4] Baumann 2004, p. 891; own translation

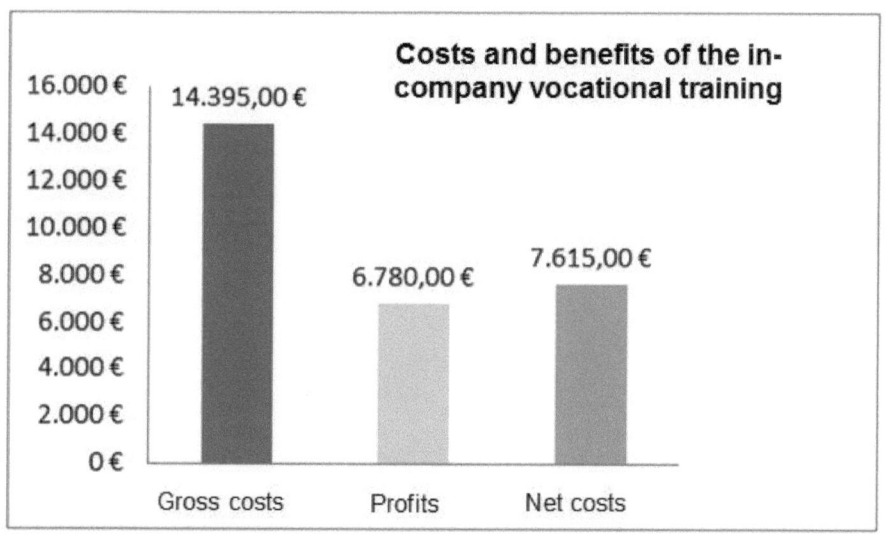

Source: Bundesinstitut für Berufsbildung

The personnel costs of the trainees, i.e. the remuneration including statutory, tariff and voluntary social benefits, are the half of the total gross educational expenditures. Beside personnel costs the companies invest in material and equipment costs (for example, workplace), in teaching materials, perhaps external courses and registration as well as examination fees. The gross expenditures of the companies can be represented as follows:

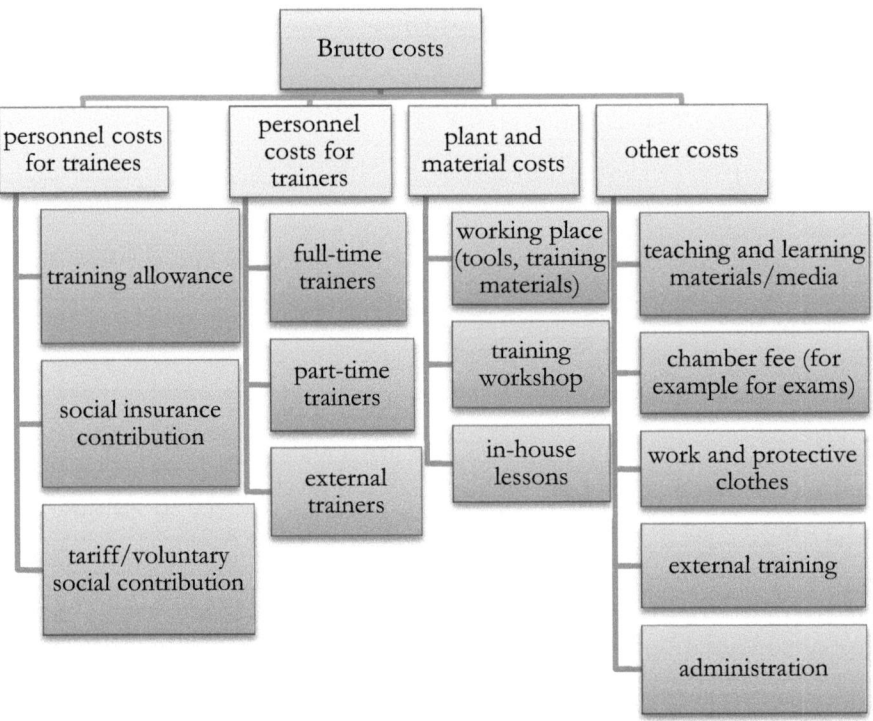

Source: Harald Pfeifer (et al.), *Kosten und Nutzen der betrieblichen Berufsausbildung,* Abschlußbericht Forschungsprojekt 2.1.203, Bundesinstitut für Berufsbildung, Bonn, December 2009, p. 9; own Translation

The educational costs of the companies are confronted by a range of advantages. For example, in comparison to the recruitment of external teaching staff own education incurs comparatively lower costs. The costs are also avoided through wrong choice or vacant posts.

2.6. Educational reasons for companies

In total about a quarter of all companies in Germany provide vocational training at the moment. Thereby the training rate (share of training companies in the total number of companies) increases with the size of the company. However, the division of trainees according to the class of the company size shows that the small and medium-sized enterprises offer the lion's share of training places[5].

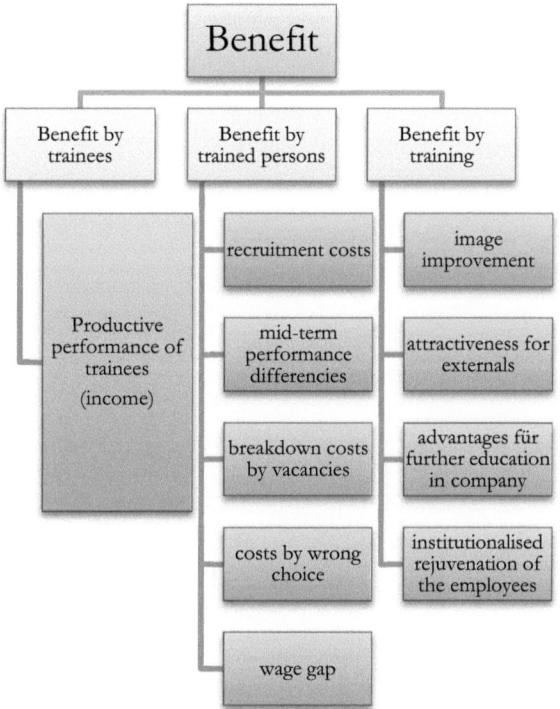

Source: Pfeifer 2009, p. 10; own translation

---

[5] Bundesministerium für Bildung und Forschung (BMBF), July 2015, p. 18

Since 1999 the number of in-company training places has dramatically decreased. Thereby a "training gap" appeared because the officially registered demand for in-company training places at the same time has decreased only to a smaller extent. However within the framework of the so-called "Training pact" it could be achieved that the number of newly concluded training contracts has increased again till 2007[6].

The apprehension that the economic crisis of the last years would cause serious cuts in the professional education has not come to reality. Indeed the offer of training places by the enterprises has decreased in 2009 by approximately 10 % in comparison to 2007; however this decline was compensated by the downward swing of demand caused by demographic reasons. Actually the offer of in-company vocational training places is significantly higher than the demand[7].

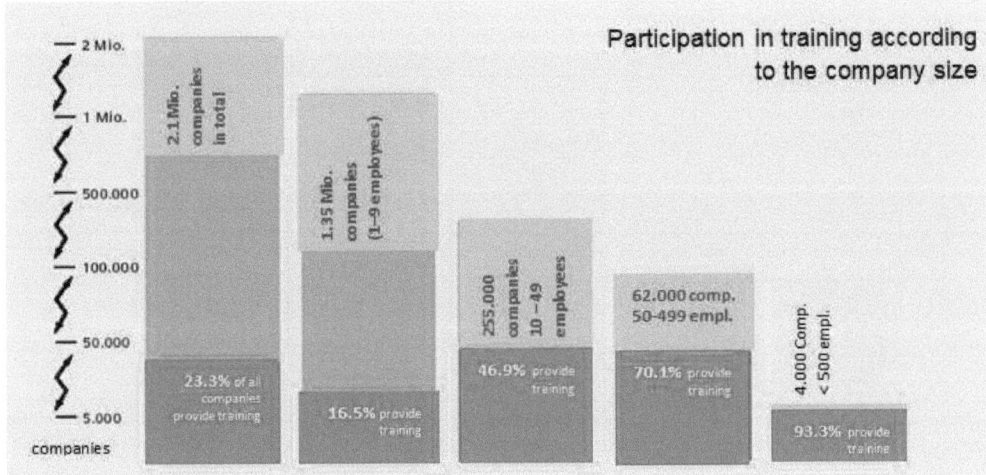

Source: Bundesministerium für Bildung und Forschung, July 2015, p. 18

---

[6] Pfeifer 2009, p. 7

[7] Schönfeld, G./Wenzelmann, F., Pfeifer, H., Dionisius, R., *Betriebliche Berufsausbildung: Ergebnisse der Kosten- und Nutzenerhebung 2007*, in: Bundesinstitut für Berufsbildung (Hrsg.): Datenreport zum Berufsbildungsbericht 2009. Informationen und Analysen zur Entwicklung der beruflichen Bildung, Bielefeld 2009, p. 230 - 242

The benefit of education for the companies consists of a variety of different elements which can only partly be assessed in monetary terms. In 2007 the Federal Institute for Vocational Training conducted a research and asked the enterprises about reasons for providing in-house training and the value of benefit. The statement that the company provides training to qualify young specialists meeting specific company requirements was by far the most popular answer, with a share of 84 %. Large segments of the sample also agreed with the following statements, indicating that enterprises are very interested in hiring their trainees following completion of training and in providing high-quality training[8]:

- Enterprise provides in-company vocational training in order to be able to choose "the best" trainees to retain (70%),
- Enterprise provides in-company vocational training in order to avoid hiring the wrong person when recruiting workers from outside (60%)

By comparison, reducing familiarization costs (34%), saving the cost of recruiting outside personnel (27%) and using company-trained employees to familiarize new employees (22%) are of less importance.

---

[8] Ibid.

Chart 6
Importance of reasons for providing in-company vocational training (in %)[12]

Source: BIBB 2007 Cost-Benefit Survey

Besides, the results of the survey show that enterprises generally benefit from providing in-company vocational training for youths. Although enterprises bear numerous costs as a result of providing training, these costs can be compensated for by retaining trainees upon completion of their training, thus eliminating the costs of externally recruiting and familiarizing new skilled workers. The costs are also offset by other less easily quantified factors such as image gains. At any rate, one third of the enterprises generate positive net gains by putting their trainees to productive use. The majority of firms surveyed are satisfied with the balance between costs and benefits, only 11% are dissatisfied. The majority also view positively their ability to meet their training needs by providing dual vocational training. More than half of the enterprises surveyed said they were satisfied with the dual vocational training system, while only some 14% were not[9].

---

[9] Schönfeld, G. (et al.) 2009, 232 - 240

2.7. Strong points of the dual vocational training system

The practice-oriented training of specialists in the dual system has lead Germany to the economic success and has contributed to its international reputation. The strong points of the system have been already discussed in the previous chapters and can be summarized as follows:

- In Germany the vocational training is firmly anchored in the society and has a high reputation. It prepares young people for a large spectrum of professions.

- The professional qualification certificates obtained in this system are still valued at the labor market and the system has remained flexible enough in order to take care of elimination of unsatisfying educational programs and to answer to the appearance of new economic and professional fields with the development of new educational programs.

- The dual system in Germany is developed especially well and combines learning at the enterprise with learning in school in order to prepare the trainees for the successful transition to the labor world. It results in the fact that the unemployment among young people in the international comparison is very low. The special pedagogy of the schooling part of the dual system is strongly oriented at solving problems and combines theory and practice in the innovative manner.

- There are fewer and fewer qualified specialists at the labour market. The one, who provides vocational training to own specialists, becomes independent from the labor market, remains competitive and retains appropriate personnel at the enterprise for a long time.

- An especially important feature of the dual system is the fact that young people are already at a very early stage exposed to the social competences, which are of critical importance for the professional success. To learn how to work in differently composed teams, to resolve conflicts with the superiors or colleagues, to treat customers or embrace an initiative and to solve problems in several steps – these are the competences, which hardly can be learnt in the classroom only.

- Training also contributes to qualification at the enterprise itself, as enterprises providing vocational training always stay up to date with technologies.

- A high identification of employees with the company leads to lower personnel change and reduces costs related to the fluctuation.

- Thanks to the time of training in the dual system it is possible for the employer to obtain information about the quality and the productivity of his young specialists relatively cost-effectively, and that enables him to appoint trainees specifically after their training or to part ways with them without having to take the risk of employing the wrong person later. The average net costs of training of young people are opposed by costs related to the search for a trained external expert, which are not incurred. In addition to that during the time of learning the company has the chance to compensate any drawbacks in the knowledge of the future specialists through targeted instruction at times and to transfer training, which is advantageous for the enterprise.

- Due to the nationwide acknowledgement and comparability of dual graduation certificates there is an advantage for the trainees, as they can utilize their education at other enterprises despite a high share of company-specific knowledge.

- Additionally, the dual education system offers the possibility to obtain a tertiary educational qualification after the completed vocational training. So it is possible that the graduates obtain a high-school entrance qualification at a vocational school without a high school diploma.

- One of the greatest advantages of the dual system is the high level of active engagement of employers and other social partners. The system is also characterized by a complex network of checks and balances at the level of the federation, of the federal states, of the community and the company. Thereby it is guaranteed that more common educational political and economic goals of the vocational training system are not suppressed by short-term needs on the part of employers. A positive influence in the dual system has also the clear division of tasks between the federation, states and the private sector, which is anchored at the statutory level and was prudently developed further throughout the years.

- The financial allocation for the vocational training system is generally good, whereby private and public financing is added to support not only the dual system and the vocational full-time schools, but also a broad range of transition programs for young people who require additional help before they can start vocational training. Despite the economic recession the vocational training system in Germany obtained further strong financial support and the employers have maintained the offer of vocational training places in order to react to the rise of unemployment among young people and in some cases also in order to avoid the threatening future personnel bottlenecks as a result of the demographic change.

- Within the dual system the chambers have a strong position. This takes some burden off the state, supports the responsibility of the economy, enables practice-oriented and company-related solutions and generally strengthens the economic self-management.

- On the federal level Germany has a research institution with high reputation, the BIBB (Federal Institute for Vocational Training) and also a nationwide network of smaller research centers, which study different aspects of the vocational training system. As a result Germany invests much more in formative research for the promotion of continuing innovation and improvement process than other countries. This is another indication of the priority attributed to the vocational training in Germany, and it makes the essential contribution to the success of the German vocational training system.

2.8. Weak points of the German vocational training system

Despite many strong points, which the German vocational training system has, there are also several challenges, which shall be primarily considered within the transfer of experiences. Thereby among other things one should mention the following points:

- The quality of cooperation between vocational schools and employers providing vocational training is improvable. Within the framework of the survey of companies providing vocational training the cooperation was considered to be very important, however the companies indicated that the cooperation is too low in practice and is often limited only to the exchange of information.

- Due to the quickly changing requirements in the world of work the educational profiles must be timely updated. Besides it is important to establish new professions to be trained on an ongoing basis and according to the demand.

- In view of the young age at which the students in Germany are expected to make a decision concerning the profession it is extremely important that everyone has access to the high-quality information and consulting. The quality of vocational counseling varies strongly in Germany.

- The assessment of the students in the dual system after the completion of the vocational training is performed using, first of all, the vocational final examination conducted by the chambers and determining whether one obtains their vocational training completion certificate (apprenticeship diploma, certificate of proficiency etc.). The study records at vocational schools are not considered officially at the vocational training final examination. This should not lead to the fact that students neglect training at vocational schools. This risk is low due to the fact that teachers from vocational schools are still members of the examination commission.

- The economic vulnerability of vocational training offers can be a problem. Nevertheless Germany always succeeded in provision of sufficient vocational training places – even during economically difficult times with very high number of school graduates in the 1980 years.

2.9. Trends and consequences for vocational education[10]

Demographics

An important challenge in Germany and all other European countries is the demographic change leading to a higher rate of older groups in comparison to younger groups, which at the same time are shrinking. The age group of less than 30 years relevant for the education will decrease from the present 25.5 million to 21.3 million in the year 2025.

Till 2025 the population in the working age will decrease from 54.1 million by 10 % to 48.8 million. At the same time the age groups of those of 65 years old or

---

[10] Jürgen Hogeforster, Lucyna Döding, *The educational systems in the Baltic Sea Region with special consideration of the dual system in Germany*, in: Job Market Innovations – testing and implementation of new methods of the promotion the employment in the niching, perishing and little popular occupations, Hamburg 2012.

older will increase from 16.7 million in 2008 to 20.2 million, or by 21% in the year 2025.

As shown in the following table these changes in the age structure of the population will continue after 2025 according to the same trend and partly also even stronger and they will represent huge challenges for the education.

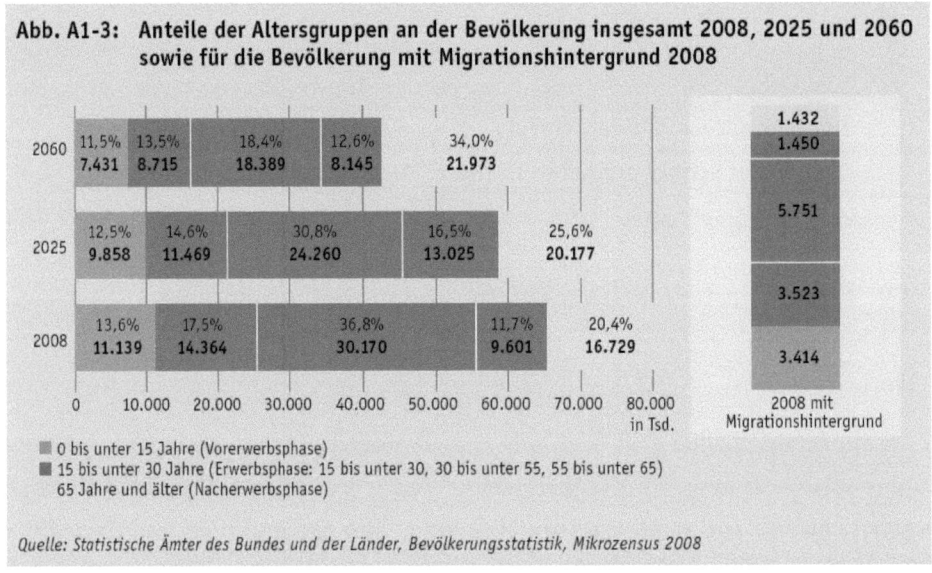

These demographic developments lead to employers having fewer apprenticeship applicants to choose from. Besides it leads to the competition between individual branches of economy (industry, crafts, administration, universities). First of all, there is danger for the crafts of not attracting enough young specialists and being pushed back to lower qualification levels.

In addition the demographic change means that in view of a smaller number of enrollers for the vocational training it will be even more important to utilize the potential of every young man and to ensure that everyone gets his chance to study a profession.

Structural change, globalization and skill levels

In the past decades a structural change could be observed in the German economy. The services sector expanded while the economic significance of other branches (agriculture and forestry, manufacturing industry) has clearly decreased. While in 1970 about 48 % of gross added value belonged to the services sector, in the year 2009 it was already 73 %.

As a result of the structural change and of the technical progress the fields of activity and thereby the requirement profiles of the working population have changed in almost all the sectors and professional fields. While manual skills have lost their significance, in the society of services and knowledge such competencies as computer knowledge and communication skills are in greater demand.

The German economy is very strongly incorporated in the world market. In the year 2007 Germany was ranked the first among the exporting states with the share of about 10 % of the world export of the goods. In 2009 as well, together with China, Germany was a leader among the exporters of goods. Approximately a quarter of all the working population employed in Germany depend on export.

Internationalization and globalization have repercussions for the system of education, as it also affects the activities and requirements profiles shaped by the structural change and the technological progress. These developments lead to a lower demand for low-qualified workers and strengthen the need for well-trained professionals. The transfer of international qualifications such as e.g. language skills or understanding of foreign markets and enterprise structures must be given stronger consideration in the future.

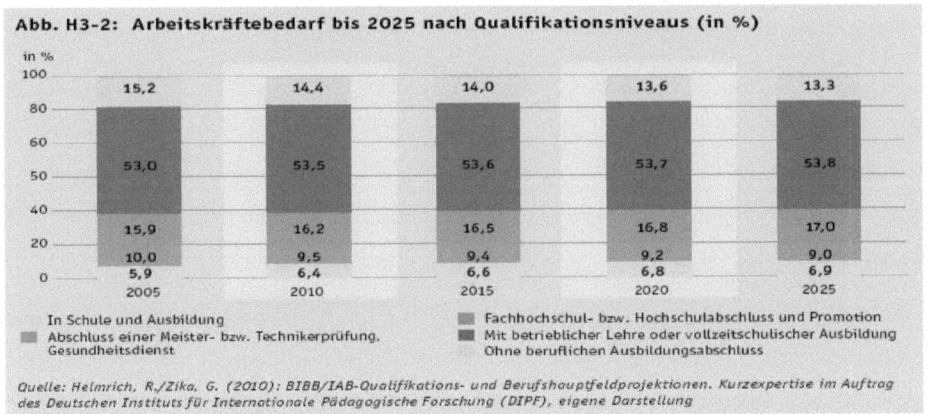

If one observes the demand in the labor market in terms of labor forces dependence on the qualifications level, the chart shows that in the following years there will be a decrease of low-qualified works and an increase of highly qualified activities. The labor forces with a graduation certificate from the dual or in the schooling vocational training system will hardly see a change in their share in the total of working population and it will be by far the largest qualification group, accounting for half of the employees.

2.10. Theses on consequences for Baltic Sea Region[11]

Opportunities for the future Baltic Sea Region

The Baltic Sea Region is deemed the most innovative and economically strong region of Europe which has not exploited its potential yet. At the same time, however, there is the emergence of revolutionary developments which can strongly limit the

---

[11] Max Hogeforster (ed.), *Objectives and strategies for education policies in the Baltic Sea Region,* Baltic Sea Academy, Volume 2, Hamburg 2012.

economic dynamics of the Baltic Sea Region and which require an increased commitment, especially in terms of educational policy. Accordingly, one of the five ambitious goals of the EU strategy "Europe 2020" is education.

Changes in labor markets

Such an evolution of educational policy is the key to the design of a fulfilling life and the social integration of each young person. Such improvements are also prominent in the interest of the economy which faces a completely different labour market situation.

Quantitative and qualitative constraints

In the next 20 years, the number of employed persons in all the Baltic States with the exception of Sweden will decrease by 5 - 20 per cent. The quantitative problems cause a substantial intensification of qualitative constraints. The requirements of companies towards trainees are high and still increasing. Personal and social skills are equally important to the factual knowledge. In most Baltic Sea States an increasing number of graduates lack the required competences.

Increased competition

There is a growing competition for skilled young people among SMEs, large enterprises, universities/colleges and government agencies. Moreover, small and medium-sized enterprises, which provide about 70per cent of jobs, threaten that they become losers and are pushed towards lower levels. Securing trainees with good qualifications and high level of innovation is a question of survival for SMEs in the Baltic Sea Region.

Local employment potential and immigration

Increased immigration to the Baltic Sea Region is required; attractive educational offers are a crucial factor here. The society must open up and meet the multicultural challenges. Above all, the domestic potential should be exploited in a better way. Educational policy must ensure that the proportion of young people leaving school without qualifications as well as non-trainable adolescents is reduced significantly. No young person should be excluded, everyone deserves a second chance.

Holistic education

The overvaluation of purely intellectual ideals of education has to be contrasted with the eminent character of education which appeals to all sensed and encourages the acquisition of all intellectual, artistic and manual skills equally. School education always seems to lead to more uniformity. Much more individualized instruction with personal learning objectives and success is urgently needed.

Promoting weaker learners and strong learners

Such holistic education with a promotion of individual talents is needed urgently for both weaker and stronger learners. An elite education is not sufficiently pronounced in many countries and it should no longer be a taboo. Systematic promotion of the strongest without the exclusion of the weakest is the decisive factor for the integration for all.

Increasing attractiveness and quality in vocational education

The attractiveness of vocational training has decreased very sharply in all Baltic States and in some countries it reached a proportion of 10-15 per cent of graduates going through vocational training, which is an alarmingly low level. The proportion of practice in vocational education must be increased significantly, especially in countries with school systems. Wherever possible, training should take place in the dual system.

Admission requirements and differentiation

The introduction of uniform Baltic Sea Region entrance requirements of vocational training which is determined job-specifically is desirable. Specific ways of vocational education need to be introduced with complete transparency for children with learning difficulties but also for stronger learners.

Openness and transparency of the educational system

Vocational education is too separated from other branches of education and quickly leads to dead ends. A complete transparency in vocational education as well as between vocational education, general education and university education with smooth transitions and recognition possibilities is urgently needed. This includes also the Baltic-wide right to study with fellowship or specialist degree, following the example of some Baltic States.

Open up for employees outside the profession

Small and medium sized business, particularly the craft sector, must open up more strongly for employees outside the profession and to win them over to a permanent employment. Tailor made teaching phase, precise further education as well as opening of the education systems and improvement of the permeability support this process.

Dual degree courses of study

Young people avoid vocational training and prefer studies. However, most coursed are largely theoretical and not sufficiently focused on the practical issues of SMEs, which cannot obtain a sufficient number of entrepreneurs and skilled workers despite a large number of students. Dual courses of study which combine vocational training or activity with studies have to be established on a broad basis.

International exchange

Stays abroad during training and professional activities promote increasingly important international knowledge and experience, and at the same time personal and social skills. The Baltic-wide un-bureaucratic recognition of vocational training and further training qualifications is a crucial prerequisite.

Educational and regional economic policy

Moreover, the reduced transport and communication costs increase the mobility of production factors. Companies migrate to locations with higher potential of professionals and workers, to locations with attractive educational opportunities and diverse labour markets. The local competition for (highly) skilled workers is more intense. A uniform educational policy in the Baltic Sea Region has to be anchored in the EU Baltic Sea strategy and ensure that this competition takes place not only within the Baltic Sea Region; to the contrary, through excellent education it strengthens the competitiveness of the whole Baltic Sea Region towards other regions and expands the existing projections.

Highest priority for the educational policy

The considerable opportunities of the Baltic Sea Region can only be exploited at the highest level of innovation and excellent qualifications. Educational policy is also to a large extent connected with locational, regional and spatial planning policy.

Education promotes innovations and competitiveness and includes the main support task for small and medium-sized enterprises. Educational policy must therefore be superior to all other policies and needs to enjoy highest priority also in the EU Baltic Sea Strategy. In accordance with the EU strategy "Europe 2020" politics, economy and society of the Baltic Sea Region must address their outstanding position of educational policy and recognize that the investment in human capital is the safest and the most profitable investment.

3. Integration of slower learner into vocational education and training system

There have been popping up numerous terms in the European Union in the last few years describing young people which build one of the risk groups on the labour market: at-risk youth, hard-to-reach learners, slower learners, "market disadvantaged" young people, etc. One thing is common these all terms; in fact these are young people who do miss a successful education and training carrier. The consequences for the individual are devastating. Leaving education and training early or not beginning it at all creates a higher risk of unemployment, jobs with less employment security, more part-time work, and lower earnings[12].

According to the latest Eurostat figures[13]:

- 5.5 million young people are still unemployed in the EU, a rate of 23.4 % (July 2013, EU28), compared to 22.9 % in July 2012 (EU27).
- The youth unemployment rate in the EU-27 has been around twice as high as the rate for the total population (end 2008), and has dramatically increased over the last four years.
- At the end of 2012 the youth unemployment rate was 2.6 times the total rate.
- One in seven young people in Europe leave the formal education system without the necessary competences and qualifications for successful labour market entry. They leave without completing upper secondary education, the level considered the minimum required for active participation in the knowledge-based economy[14].

The total of young people not in employment, education or training, is currently around 14 million in the EU. The annual economic loss to society is estimated at

---

[12] European Commission/EACEA/Eurydice/Cedefop, *Tackling Early Leaving from Education and Training in Europe: Strategies, Policies and Measure,* Eurydice and Cedefop Report. Luxembourg: Publications Office of the European Union, 2014, p. 21.

[13] Eurostat: http://ec.europa.eu/eurostat

[14] CEDEFOP Research Paper, *Guiding At-risk Youth through Learning to Work Lessons from across Europe*, Luxembourg: Publications Office of the European Union, 2010 p. 12

€162 billion (Eurofound, 2013), in addition to the long term personal and social costs[15].

This "at-risk" youth show up heterogeneous reasons for their failure in the existing education and training systems, where they leave the (secondary) school education without school diploma, cannot start vocational training or end up in long queues:

- socioeconomic background,
- poor basic skills,
- learning difficulties in the school based education system,
- cultural background,
- external environment

to list few of them. Moreover, young people who are not in education, employment or training are disproportionately likely to have experienced poor attainment at school, low motivation, truancy, homelessness, and poverty, lack of family support, health problems, special educational needs, disabilities or unemployment in the family. Many have had negative experiences of school and faced issues such as bullying, exclusion, behavioural difficulties, and stress. Some young people from relatively poor backgrounds find it difficult to progress into further education or training as they struggle to cope financially or they feel pressure to begin contributing to family finances. For some young people, finding an opportunity to earn money, by whatever means, becomes a priority over continuing their education or training[16].

---

[15] Expert Group Report, *Developing the Creative and innovative Potential of Young People through Non-formal Learning in Ways that are Relevant to Employability,* European Commission 20.11.2012, COM (2012) 669, p. 10: http://ec.europa.eu/youth/library/reports/creative-potential_en.pdf (June 2014).

[16] CEDEFOP 2010, pp. 25 – 26

However, failure at school and dropping out of the education system is a complex bunch of factors. Besides, the individual attitudes like listed above, the following ones play also an important role: "[…]school environment (physical, social, school atmosphere) and the teaching staff (expectations, style of delivery, understanding of the needs of and experience in working with marginalised groups) play a part in raising aspirations and supporting school completion. Further, a significant proportion of young people leave school early as a result of disaffection with the system, skills limitations (such as poor basic skills) or due to the lack of availability of alternative forms of learning opportunities. […]The Community Health Systems Resource Group (2005) supports this perspective by identifying that early school leaving is typically not based on a single decision made at a specific moment"[17].

The individual failure in the education and VET systems is just the one side of the coin. The other one is that structural change is needed to meet the needs of youth and the labour markets in the EU. Moreover, the attractiveness of vocational education and training must be increased. So, in individual countries like in Latvia increasing attractiveness has been even set as one of the policy priorities for education[18].

In this context, work-based learning shall replace the existing "outdated" VET systems. The structural change as condition develops high-quality work-based learning and strong apprenticeship systems, involving long-term commitment by employers and policymakers. The benefits for individuals, enterprises and indeed society at large are significant[19]. Work-based learning is an example of a win-win situation[20].

---

[17] CEDEFOP 2010, p. 26

[18] CEDEFOP, *Vocational education and training in Latvia: Short description,* Luxembourg: Publications Office of the European Union. Cedefop information series, 2015, p. 32

[19] European Commission, Education and Training, *Work-based Learning in Europe: Practices and Policy Pointers,* Brussels June 2013, p. 32, http://ec.europa.eu/education/policy/vocational-policy/doc/alliance/work-based-learning-in-europe_en.pdf (July 2015)

[20] European Commission 2013, p. 7

The education reforms have taken, and are taking place across Europe to transform education and training systems, to meet better the needs of young people who have already dropped out or are at risk of doing so. Such reforms have included, for example, the creation of alternative learning options, the development of more comprehensive and tailored delivery methods, widening choices, providing better and more targeted support, addressing barriers to participation, and making practical changes such as tracking young people more effectively[21].

Although in comparison to former Soviet countries in Germany and the Nordic countries the vocational pathway continues to be regarded as a high status route into employment and the youth unemployment is comparably low, there are undertaken numerous measures to enable access to vocational education and training for as many young people as possible and especially involving the "at-risk" youth. One of such measures that was started 2010 in Hamburg is the so called Hamburg Model or Hamburg Model. This model of the dual education system integrates young people successfully into vocational training. So, for example, more than 75% of all participating students in the Hamburg Model in the school year 2011/2012 in Hamburg completed the vocational qualification successfully and concluded a vocational training contract[22].

The Hamburg Model is a proven method to integrate young people into the professional education, who would otherwise not get this chance. This is why the model was taken as pattern to be adapted to other countries and transferred. In the following chapter the Hamburg Model is presented in detail.

---

[21] CEDEFOP 2010, p. 8
[22] Radder, E. / Rominger, M., *Report of the Working Group 'Vocational Qualification'*, Draft – State as of 20 September 2012 3:00 pm, Hamburg Institut für Berufliche Bildung (HIBB), September 2012, p. 7

4. Hamburg Model

The following detailed description of the Hamburg Model bases on a part of the framework concept prepared by J. E. Radder, Hamburg Institute for Vocational Education (Hamburg Institut für Berufliche Bildung) from 24.06.2010: Part Project 3 – Hamburg Model (Teilprojekt 3 – Hamburger Ausbildungsmodell).

4.1. Framework concept

Objectives

The Hamburg Model (HM) with the professional qualification (PQ) as the first training element or the first year of training upon condition of fulfillment of admission prerequisites offers direct access to the vocational training at the following learning locations: vocational schools, at enterprises and education providers, if necessary also at corporate training centers. Young people are trained in recognized training occupations according to the Vocational Training Act (BBiG), Crafts Code (HwO) or according to the state law, the duration can be two, three or three and a half years of education according to the training occupation. The training has to be provided in professions for which

- there is a demand in specialists at the labour market,
- the target group of the HM fulfills the admission prerequisites of the dual vocational training and
- the needs of this cooperative training model can be satisfied, namely training places at enterprises have to be available.

But still the vocational training in the dual vocational training system which is not promoted has the priority.

Within the framework of the reform of the transition system "School – Profession" the HM follows the resolutions of the Study Commission "Consequences of the new PISA study for the Hamburg school development" and also the standards of the government program dated April 17, 2008. Its goal is to reduce queues within the framework of the reform of the transition system "School – Profession" through creditable compatible and easy-to-complete professional qualification of high school graduates and also to strengthen the dual vocational training.

Target groups and admission prerequisites

The HM is the training offer for young people which have not found their training opportunity in the dual vocational training system despite the training maturity and the available multiple application attempts. In the PQ, the first training year of the HM, <u>school age young people</u> who reached training maturity are admitted; as a rule they are graduates of district schools who will not succeed or haven't succeeded to make a transition to the dual vocational training at the end of the 10th school attendance year (so called "market disadvantaged" young people).

A participant is identified as having reached training maturity if he/she possesses the general features of educational and working capacity and also has all the minimum attributes to start the vocational training. Thereby specific requirements of separate professions which are used for the evaluation of fitness for the corresponding profession (vocational aptitude) are not taken into account. Training maturity which is absent at the moment (e.g. at the moment of application to the place in the PQ) does not rule out the fact that it can be achieved at a later moment – during the PQ (see also: National Pact for Career Training and Skilled Manpower Development in Germany, criteria catalogue for the training maturity, page 13). Within the framework of the application procedure the vocational school determines the training maturity; thereby it is guided by the cited criteria catalogue for the training maturity.

The foundation for this orientation is built also by certificates of the district school in conjunction with the vocational and training courses plan. The generic competences[23] of school children which have to be assigned to the field of personnel competence are evaluated there:

    a. Persistence / patience

    b. Determination

    c. Commitment

    d. Self-confidence / self-efficacy

    e. Independence / self-organization

    f. Frustration tolerance / perseverance

    g. Communicative ability

    h. Cooperation ability / ability to work in a team

    i. Ability to take criticism

    j. Ability to accept rules / manners

    k. Sense of responsibility

    l. Reliability

---

[23] The terms and their definitions are being currently coordinated with the Land Institute / Educational Plan Development, the Department B of the BSB and the Hamburg Economy.

4.2. Hamburg Model with professional qualification

The HM is structured in the PQ as the first year of training and – if the training is not continued with a vocational training contract at the enterprise – in the provider-supported vocational training with a vocational training contract in the second, the third and the fourth years. Thereby the HM is integrated in the dual vocational training system:

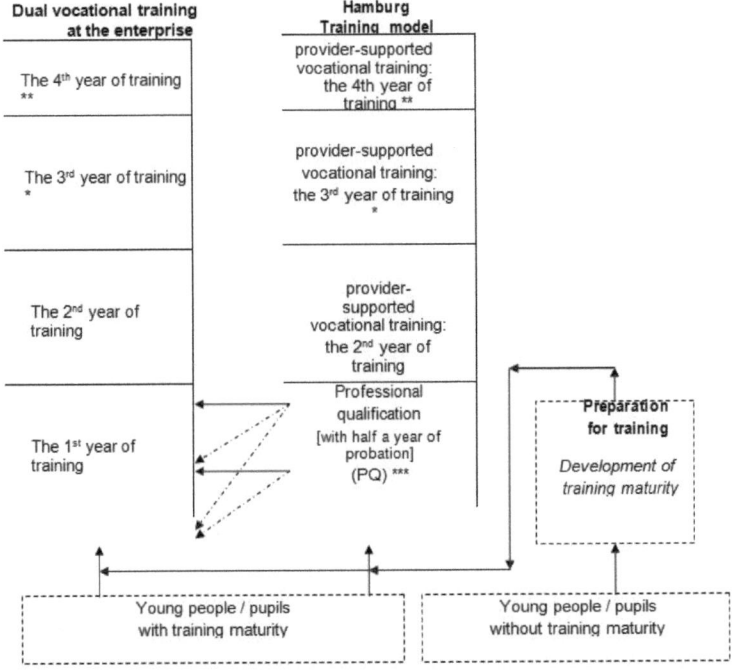

* during 3-year and 3½-year vocational trainings

** during 3½-year vocational trainings

*** Transition to vocational training at an enterprise with or without the acknowledgement of PQ training contents

Choice of suitable professions

The choice of professions, which correspond to the prerequisites and abilities of the target group and are in demand at the labour market, is made with the help of six criteria:

1. In the economy **there is** a demand for trained specialists in this profession. The transition to this work is secured with high probability or it is at least easy to manage.

2. It is a profession for which the demand for specialists is expected also in the future.

3. The transition to the vocational training is evaluated as positive. This applies not only during but also after the PQ also in the following provider-supported vocational training.

4. The profession is suitable for young people with training maturity and also with differentiated levels of education (young people with lower abilities with the first general education school-leaving qualification (secondary modern school qualification) and with the secondary school qualification).

5. The Hamburg enterprises are capable of offering enough places for the professional education during the PQ or for the vocational education phases during the provider-supported vocational training of the HM.

6. On the part of young people there is a demand for dual vocational training places in the offered profession.

If possible at least for the start-up phase of the HM professions should be chosen beyond these criteria which are broad in scope and allow vocational development in electronic, metal and service provision professions among others.

The identification of professions which are suitable for the HM is performed through the Hamburg Institute for Vocational Training in coordination with the agency for labour, with the office for further training, the board for school and vocational training and also responsible chambers.

In addition thereto during the choice of suitable professions the prescribed corporate training of apprentices or instructions in construction professions have to be taken into account (see Note 3.2 Professional qualification, framework conditions and organization, paragraph 8), because the communication of apprentice training contents must also be secured in the PQ.

4.3. Professional qualification

Framework conditions and organization

The <u>PQ is the training offer in the school form "Vocational school"</u>. The participants of the PQ are pupils according to the status law; they do not receive any training allowances accordingly. The weekly working and educational time at school, at the enterprise and at the corporate training facilities is guided by corresponding labour agreements. As a rule it includes 38 to 40 hours.

Concerning content and time the PQ complies with the regulatory instruments of the corresponding occupation requiring training. The PQ describes the first year of training according to the contents and time periods. The subject-related practical training should correspond to the content and timely standards of the framework plan of the training in the corresponding profession; therefore it can also take place during school holidays.

The foundation is the educational contract which determines the goals of training in the PQ, on the one part, and on the other part, determines the rights and obligations of the school and also of participants during this training phase comparable to the educational contract according to the Vocational Training Act (BBiG) or Crafts Code (HwO). The educational contract is signed between the school (school management) which provides vocational training and the participant or the persons entitled to custody.

According to the educational contract the participant of the PQ is obliged to participate regularly in the classes at the school which provides vocational training and also to participate regularly in extra-school training phases. In case of inexcusable absence the school shall apply the "Directive for dealing with violations of mandatory school attendance laws".

The above-named possibility to hold vocational training during holidays should be stipulated not only in the training and examination regulations of the PQ but also in the educational contract.

The <u>training in the PQ is performed in close cooperation with enterprises, chambers and professional associations</u>. Within the framework of cooperation between the school which provides vocational training and the enterprise the powers and responsibilities are agreed in writing. In addition thereto there is regular feedback between schools and chambers in order to evaluate possible effects on the offer of training places at the enterprises which provide places for practical training within the framework of the PQ.

The common task of the school, the enterprise and corporate training centers is to develop the occupational competence (professional, methodical, social and personal competence) of participants which is required for the achievement of the goal of training in the intended profession. The training must be performed so that the goal of training could be achieved within the provided period of training. For this purpose also rooms for practical trainings at vocational schools can be used.

The subject-related practical training takes place during vocational training phases. In the professions related to crafts and construction it should be checked in particular which prescribed (apprentice) trainings have to be completed at corporate training centers, what is the amount of funds required for the cover of costs and if workshops / rooms for practical training at schools which provide vocational training can be used alternatively.

- Concerning vocational training in professions related to crafts according to the Regulation on corporate training of apprentices (ICTA regulation) intercompany training of apprentices is prescribed. Concerning professions in the field of construction comparable training is prescribed in the trainings regulations. Trainees in these professions with the educational contract according to the Vocational Training Act (BBiG) or Crafts Code (HwO) have to visit these trainings for apprentices or courses. Because participants of the PQ are pupils and they have not concluded any educational contracts according to the BBiG or HwO, therefore the ICTA regulation is not binding. The communication of training content is though mandatory.

- If offers concerning the corporate training of apprentices at corporate training centers or courses at training centers for the construction industry are not used within the framework of the PQ, the responsible school which provides vocational training must clarify how the contents of the respective training of apprentices or the respective courses have to be communicated to the participants of the PQ in full scope. The procedure, especially the acknowledgement of communication of training contents in the school rooms for practical training has to be clarified with the responsible authorities (chambers) before the beginning of the PQ.

The <u>supervision and support of participants</u> during vocational training phases also at corporate training centers are the responsibility of the vocational training school. It includes regular visits of participants at extra-school training centers and the goal thereof is the support of participants especially in problem situations at the enterprise.

The awareness of this supervision and support by professionals outside of schools should be sought after, e.g. by the provider of the further provider-supported vocational training. The integration of the provider for the supervision and support of participants of PQ is possible within the framework of the expression-of-interest procedure for the further provider-supported vocational training in the respective profession, it determines the timely choice and determination of suitable professions (in autumn of the preceding year), in order to guarantee the supervision and the support of young people in the PQ starting from August of the following year.

The <u>classes at vocational school</u> take place if possible in mainstream classes of the respective profession. They are oriented at working and business processes of the respective training, they are held with orientation at activities and learning field and the approaches of the individual learning are taken into account. The framework curriculum of the first year of training in the respective profession has to be implemented.

The <u>holidays of the participants</u> have to be determined as agreed upon between the school and the enterprise or the enterprises for the time which is free of classes (school holidays).

Application procedure and qualifying conditions

In the PQ for the respective profession only a limited number of training places is available, and the school which provides vocational training can admit participants only for established and available training places. The qualifying conditions have to be specified in the training and examination procedure which has to be prepared as well as for the piloting (school pilot project):

- Qualifying limitations have to be foreseen for the offered professions concerning number of training places in the PQ.
- The number of training places in the PQ is limited by the number of available cooperation agreements with enterprises for the training phases at the enterprise. In addition thereto the number of training places can be limited by available work and study places e.g. at school workshops or labs.
- The limited number of training places in the PQ has to be explained and proven by the responsible school.

The admission to the PQ takes place after the application in writing with the proof of training maturity and of the competence required for the intended vocational training and also after the interview. For the application procedure applies the following:

- The moment for application is determined every year. The application is addressed with completed application documents (letter of application with the reasoning of the decision concerning the choice of profession, CV, certificates e.g. concerning studying at extracurricular learning centers) to the respective vocational training school.
- The applicant takes part in an interview. During the interview the applicant describes his/her interest in the chosen profession. He/she proves the obtained competences e.g. in a portfolio, gives reasons for the decision concerning the choice of profession and provides proof of serious failed (about 10) applications for vocational training places in the profession which are not promoted.
- The school which provides vocational training documents the whole application procedure incl. the interview.
- Incomplete application documents, not observed deadlines and not proven failed application and mediation attempts for vocational training places which are not promoted lead to rejection.

As a whole the interview in connection with the application documents creates clarity that the applicant actually has orientation at the profession and possesses training maturity. On the basis of evaluation of applications incl. interviews a rank order for the allocation of places in the PQ appears. If the training places in the PQ are not occupied by the applicants at the beginning of the school years, free places have to be given according to the succession procedure to young people who have to attend school.

If it is required for the specific profession, in addition thereto for the admission to the PQ applicants have to provide a certificate of medical examination referring to §§ 32 and 33 of the Youth Health and Safety at Work Act.

In-year admission of PQ participants should be striven for.

Performance evaluation

The performance results of participants at the PQ (i.e. of pupils) are evaluated with marks. This applies not only to separate subjects but also to practical training at the enterprise according to the educational framework plan of the corresponding training regulations.

The practical training in the specialty is evaluated by the corresponding enterprise or the corporate training center. On the basis of evaluations by the enterprise or enterprises and also by the corporate training center and also on the basis of evaluation of performance at practical training places at school at the report conference the school obtains a mark for the vocational practical training. In order to achieve an agreed and possibly uniform evaluation procedure for the vocational practical training a competence-oriented assessment sheet has been developed for the enterprises (Annex 7, Performance evaluation by the enterprise).

An accounting meeting is held with the participants and also with the persons entitled to custody after three months and before the end of the half a year probation period. As desired by the participant or by the person entitled to custody a further accounting meeting is held after three quarters of a year during which the vocational perspective after school is discussed.

The achieved performance and the obtained competences have to be documented by schools providing vocational training and also by participants in the suitable form (see Note 3.4. Documentation system related to the process and the state of vocational training, page 9).

Half a year probation period

Instead of regulated probation period according to the Vocational Training Act (BBiG) or Crafts Code (HwO) in the PQ a half a year probation period is introduced. The decision concerning the successful completion of the half a year probation period is made on the basis of marks.

The grade average for the half a year probation period without the subject "Sports" is 4,3 (in German System 1=the best grade and 6=the worst one, *Ed.*). The performance during the vocational practical training at the enterprise, in the corporate training center and – if applicable – at school which provides vocational training must be at least sufficient for the successful completion of the half a year probation period; unsatisfactory or poor performance during the vocational practical training cannot be compensated with other marks.

Securing connection

The participants at the PQ are encouraged by schools which provide vocational training to take part in yearly subsequent placement activities and they are supported thereby. Also after the subsequent placement activity the transition to vocational training which is not promoted is the explicit objective of the PQ.

The school guarantees the connection of participants to the dual vocational training at the enterprise or to the provider-supported vocational training. What concerns participants who have to attend school and leave without PQ graduation care have to be taken for their transition to a suitable further system.

If the participant wants to withdraw from the PQ before the end of the school year or he or she completes the half a year probation period unsuccessfully, in case of compulsory school attendance there is a transition to the preparation for education or measures for the preparation to the training have to be taken.

4.4. Graduation, graduation certificate, leaving

The performance results of participants with marks are indicated in certificates, and also the mark for the performance during the vocational practical training at the enterprise (or at corporate training centers or at school workshops/rooms for practical training). The performance during the school year is summarized with the year mark without the graduation examination for each subject. The PQ representatives of the enterprise and also education supervisors should participate as consultants at the report conference dedicated to the graduation.

In case of successful participation the graduation certificate in PQ is issued: the participant of the PQ obtains the graduation certificate, if in all the subjects except for the subject "Sports" he has at least sufficient performance results or poor performance results can be compensated. Poor performance results in one subject – with the exception of vocational practical training – are compensated with at least good performance results in another subject or satisfactory marks in two other subjects. Poor performance results in more than two subjects or poor performance results in the vocational practical training or unsatisfactory results cannot be compensated. If there is the subject "Sports" poor or unsatisfactory performance results remain unconsidered. [The exact formulation of conditions is presented in the educational and examination regulations]. The graduation certificate contains a supplement in which the school which provides vocational training certifies the competences and qualifications obtained by the participant.

The participants who enter the vocational training at the enterprise from the PQ prematurely obtain a school certificate with a note that the transition to the dual vocational training was achieved at the enterprise. [The exact formulation of the note is presented in the educational and examination regulations].

4.5. Continuation and completion of training

Transition to the dual vocational training at the enterprise

The goal of the PQ is the transition to the vocational training at an enterprise which is not promoted, during the PQ or after the expiry of the PQ at the latest. Thereby one should strive for the crediting of education contents of PQ. A corresponding crediting of PQ is left to the discretion of educational enterprises and of the apprentice during the transition to the training at the enterprise. The crediting is performed according to the regulations of the Vocational Training Act (BBiG) (§ 8 paragraph 1) or Crafts Code (HwO) (§ 27b paragraph 1) (compare also Annex 8, Procedure for the acknowledgement of educational contents of the PQ).

During the PQ the school and training supervisors support the participants during their search for a vocational training place which is not promoted at an enterprise and also during their application thereto.

Transition to the provider-supported vocational training

If after the expiry of the PQ the continuation of training at an enterprise is not possible, then a transition to the second year of training within the framework of publicly funded training at the education provider takes place. The crediting of the first year of training completed during the PQ is requested by the trainee and the provider at the responsible chamber.

- Before the beginning of the PQ the procedure for the acknowledgement for the training in the PQ for the following provider-supported vocational training has to be agreed and determined between the responsible school and the responsible chamber or the responsible professional association (Annex 8, Procedure for the acknowledgement of training contents of the PQ).

For the remaining duration of provider-supported vocational training an educational contract is concluded according to the Vocational Training Act (BBiG) or Crafts Code (HwO). The training allowance is set according to usual rates of publicly financed educational measures.

The training provided by the training provider is performed with the purpose to carry out the shift to the training at an enterprise. For this purpose the achieved levels of performance and the obtained competences have to be evaluated and certified in suitable form in the documents of the trainee.

The training provider documents the progress of training and the performance of the trainee.

Resources for the provider-supported vocational training

The allocation decision for the provider-supported vocational training is made on the basis of interest declaration procedure (see Annex 3, Draft interest declaration for the implementation of promoted vocational training…).

The financing of provider-supported vocational training is being currently discussed.

Documentation system related to the progress and status of vocational training

The participants of the PQ maintain a training certificate according to the Vocational Training Act (BBiG) in which the contents of the classes in the vocational training school and the vocational practical training are represented. The training certificate serves as the documentation of the training status during transition to the vocational training at an enterprise or to the provider-supported vocational training.

The training certificate is a constituent part of the portfolio which has to include evaluations of enterprises or of the school which provides vocational training related to the vocational practical training, e.g. certificates.

Within the framework of the following provider-supported vocational training the provider takes care of documentation of progress and status of training.

Quality assurance and development by schools providing vocational training and by the providers

The responsibility for the quality management is connected with the implementation of the HM, especially of PQ, for schools providing vocational training. On the basis of the framework concept "Quality assurance and development for the schools providing vocational training" (Hamburg, June 2007)

- it develops a structure which aim is to assure and develop the quality,
- it makes mandatory specifications for the evaluation of the offered profession or of the offered professions in the HM, e.g. with the registration of the effect and the results (especially of the PQ),
- it continuously develops the offer further,
- it secures the results,
- it creates the transparency concerning the performed work and reports about the implementation.

In coordination with the provider of further provider-supported vocational training the school which provides vocational training secures the quality of further education. The quality assurance for the provider-supported vocational training is also regulated by the allocation agreement.

To the data sources for the reporting system belong especially

- the issue of documentation concerning the training progress for each participant,
- the registration of current status of participants during and at the end of the PQ incl. possible termination and reasons,
- the issue of the analysis of what is left to pass for dropouts,
- the documentation of visits to extracurricular educational centers (point of time and time frame, topic/reason, result) within the framework of the PQ and also
- receiving and compiling feedback related to the course of training and performance results from enterprises or corporate training centers during the PQ, in the provider-supported vocational training or after the transition from the PQ to the vocational training at an enterprise.

As agreed upon with the Hamburg Institute for Vocational Training success criteria have to be determined for specific professions of the HM especially for the PQ.

The schools evaluate the results of the HM – within the framework of the provider-supported vocational training together with the providers – and prepare a results report. The obtained knowledge is used for the evaluation and it is the basis for the further development of the HM.

In the following chapter on the basis of the profession "Metalworkers" it is exemplary shown how the Hamburg Model can be integrated in the dual vocational training.

4.6. Hamburg Model with Professional Qualification (PQ) in the profession: Metalworkers (G 01)

1. Application procedure for the PQ (details are named in the framework concept concerning the Hamburg Model)

   - The participants have to apply for the admission to the PQ and therefore to the Hamburg Model.

   - Prerequisites for the admission are orientation at the profession or the professional field (decision concerning the choice of profession), the training maturity, proven failed applications for vocational training places at an enterprise and also completed application documents.

2. Training places in the PQ (details are named in the framework concept concerning the Hamburg Model)

   - There is a limited number of places in the PQ which is determined by the number of training places at cooperating enterprises and/or the number of places at practical training places at schools.

3. Framework conditions for the PQ

   - Funds for the organization: educational framework plan and framework curriculum for the first year of training

   - Educational contract between the school which provides vocational training and the participants in the PQ

4. Transition to the vocational training at an enterprise or provider-supported vocational training

- During or after the PQ the transition to vocational training at an enterprise is striven for, acknowledgement or reduction of training has to be striven for. A corresponding crediting of PQ is left for the discretion of vocational training enterprises in case of transition to vocational training. The crediting is performed according to the regulations of the BBiG (§ 8 paragraph 1) and the HwO (§ 27b paragraph .1)
- The transition to the provider-supported training is performed after the application for the acknowledgement of educational contents of the PQ (the first year of training) with the responsible chamber.

5. Framework conditions for the provider-supported vocational training

- regular educational contracts according to BBiG or HwO
- organizational regulations: educational framework plan and framework curriculum

Phase of training	School part of training	Vocational training			Comment
		Training at an enterprise	Vocational training at school	Corporate training	
The 1st year as professional qualification (PQ), school form: vocational school	- Vocational school in part-time form during 2 days or training in blocks as agreed upon with the enterprises - Communication of contents and development of competences according to the framework curriculum the 1. year of training - Individual support - Consulting and reflection during the learning phase at an enterprise	**Training / learning at an enterprise** - In accordance with the educational framework plan in the enterprise reality - Educational supervision by school (it guarantees correspondence concerning educational contents and provides assistance in case of difficulties with pupils).	**Days of school practice** - Vocational practice at practical training places at schools (workshops, kitchens, ...) for partial aspects or contents from the educational framework plan which cannot be covered by participating enterprises (as agreed)	**Training at corporate training centers** - corporate courses: main course in metal works, welding course with certified graduation or - alternatively communication of contents of corporate courses at practical training places at schools (if possible)	- Courses at corporate training centers are reasonable because the certificate represents already partial qualification also in case of drop out - Certificates which confirm obtained competences, if possible also in case of termination of PQ

Phase of training	School part of training	Vocational training		Comment
		Training at an enterprise	Corporate training	
the 2nd year of training	Vocational school in the 2nd year of training According to the framework plan; form of organization as agreed upon with providers and participating enterprises in blocks or part-time form	Provider / enterprise According to the educational framework plan for the 2nd year (All the scheduled corporate courses are contained in the training provided by the provider.)	according to the regulation concerning corporate training for apprentices	Apprenticeship certification exam part I after 1,5 to 2 years of training
		(no training at school)		

	Vocational school in the 3rd year of training	Provider / enterprise	
The 3rd year of training	According to the framework plan; form of organization as agreed upon with providers and participating enterprises in blocks or part-time form	According to the educational framework plan for the 3rd year (All the scheduled corporate courses are contained in the training provided by the provider.)	In case of provider-supported training guarantee of at least 12 months of (training) phases at an enterprise
	Vocational school in the 4th year of training	**Provider / enterprise**	according to the regulation concerning corporate training for apprentices
The 4th year of training	According to the framework plan; form of organization as agreed upon with providers and participating enterprises in blocks or part-time form	According to the educational framework plan for the 4th year (All the scheduled corporate courses are contained in the training provided by the provider.)	Final examination / Apprenticeship certification exam

5. Implementation of the Hamburg Model in Lithuania and Hungary

During the project the Hamburg Model was adapted to the country conditions in Lithuania and Hungary and piloted there succesfully. In Lithuania the Vilnius Builders Training Center and in Hungary the Kontiki and the TANEXT Akadémia Vocational School provided the training. The following both chapters describe the implementation of the Hamburg Model in these both countries and shall serve as practice examples for adaption and implementation of the Hamburg Model in two different countries, where the introduction of work-based learning i.a. of the dual vocational education elements are waiting in the wings.

The both pilots were accompanied by evelution that was carried out by external evaluators: Gediminas Technical University in Vilnius and Corvinus University of Budapest. The summarised evaluation reports of both countries complete this part of the book.

5.1. Implementation of the Hamburg Model in Lithuania[24]

Background information:

> ➢ Programme title: *Building insulation worker*

---

[24] The implementation report for Lithuania has been prepared by Renata Černeckienė, Vilnius Builders Training Centre, June 2015, Vilnius.

- Duration of training: *01.09.2014 – 30.06.2015*

- No. of trainees: 16 (7 young workers already acting in the labour market but without having any or required qualification and 9 trainees with lower academic achievements but rather good practical skills)

- Delivery of theoretical training:

    Vilnius Builders Training Centre, Laisvės pr. 53, Vilnius 07191, LT

    Responsible trainers: Alma Briedienė, Vytautas Nekrošius

- Delivery of practical training:

    UAB „Fasadų apšiltinimo sistemos" (Joint stock company „Facade insulation systems"), Rinktinės g. 55-22, Vilnius 09207, LT

    Responsible mentor: Vidas Staveckas

Aims and objectives

The main objective of the training was that at least 70% of participants should continue working in the construction industry in the field of the acquired qualification (thermal insulation of buildings) or continue their studies in vocational education.

Contents of Training

The contents of the training were selected, developed and adapted by the school trainers in close cooperation with the company, taking into account the employers' requirements and current demands of the labour market. The main aim of the training was to have qualified workers possessing sufficient knowledge and skills for performance of thermal insulation works.

The training programme was composed of the following training modules:

- Occupational health and safety;
- Reading of technical drawings;
- Building materials and products;
- Basics of brick- and concrete-laying;
- Woodworking using manual tools;
- Building insulation;
- Plastering;
- Tiling;
- Painting;
- Fixing plaster-board panels;
- Fixing decorative panels and linear elements;
- Fixing exterior building elements;
- Basics of green construction.

The total number of training hours was 1480 which was sub-divided as follows:

- *480 hours* for theoretical training (performed at Vilnius Builders Training Centre),
- *1000 hours* for practical training (performed at the construction company).

School-based training

Implementation of the training programme started on September 1st, 2014, with an introductory course delivered at Vilnius Builders Training Centre. During the time spent at school the trainees acquired the background knowledge and basic skills that they could later use in real work situations. Theoretical training at school also included necessary clarifications and review after the in-company training.

The training schedule was arranged in such a way that the trainees would spent 2 weeks at school and then go for a longer practical training period (approx. 4 weeks) to the company.

Assesment and evaluation were performed with regard to the usual practice of the school (i.e. trainers writing marks for each subject after completing a certain part of the course). The average mark for theory for the whole group was *8.5* (in Lithuania the lowest positive mark is 4 and the highest is 10).

The attendance rate was rather high as well - *94,3%* for the whole group.

Theoretical training and acquiring basic skills in insulation:

In-company training

The practical training in the company was based on real work situations at 2 construction sites in Vilnius. The training focused on the two main areas:

1) Insulation and finishing with decorative plastering (a newly built, 5 floor residential building);

2) Installing ventilated facades (a 5 floor block of flats, built in 1990, now undergoing rehabilitation).

The trainees worked full time (8 hours/day) under constant supervision and assistance of the company mentor (his position in the company is a site manager).

Main activities during in-company training:

- The trainees were introduced to Occupational Health and safety rules, including the use of Personal Protection Equipment, and had to confirm their compliance by signing in the Occupational Health and safety register.

- They were also instructed on fire prevention, how to react in case of fire, and signed the required documentation.

- Then they were introduced to the construction sites and the objects to be insulated.

- Before starting any work activity, the trainees had to get acquainted and sign the form of "Technology of the working process".

- Each on-site training activity was divided into phases, starting with simple steps, requiring basic skills, and going into a more complicated process, including numerous operations and technologies.

- Assesment and evaluation: the trainees' performance at the construction site was continually monitored and corrected, suggesting areas for improvement as well as acknowledging successes. The company mentor completed the register provided by the school, writing marks for every trainee. The average mark for practice for the whole group was 9,2. The attendance rate was 96,4% for the whole group.

- Wages paid to all trainees from the 2nd month of work (200-250 Euros, the amount depending on the performance of each individual trainee). This could be pointed out as a special achievement of the project because the usual practice in Lithuania is that the trainees are not paid during the practice time.

- Main skills and competences acquired: fixing various building insulation systems, application of main finishing techniques, compliance with Health and Safety requirements, basics of green construction, etc.

A group of trainees at practical training activities on the construction site:

Final qualification examinations

Final qualification examinations took place on June 16-17th, 2015. They consisted of theoretical and practical parts and were organized at a sectoral practical training centre based at Vilnius Builders Training Centre. The tasks were prepared and as-assessment was performed by the external body (*Chambers of Crafts*) in collaboration with the school teachers and company representatives.

The examples of a theory test and a practical task (in Lithuanian language) are annexed to this report.

The average assessment for theoretical part was *8.56*.

The average assessment for practical performance was *9.13*.

The documented assessment results are annexed to the report.

Main findings and achievements:

➢ The proposed training model has been successfully implemented and is suitable for Lithuanian VET system. The general opinion and feedback provided by the involved trainees, trainers and company staff are quite positive.

The only problematic aspect that has been highlighted by all the participant parties was the duration of the training programme. One year is definitely not enough to for the implementation of the dual training model.

> The main aim set at the beginning of the implementation has been achieved with the majority of the students having chosen to stay in the company (9 trainees) or to continue with VET studies (4 trainees):

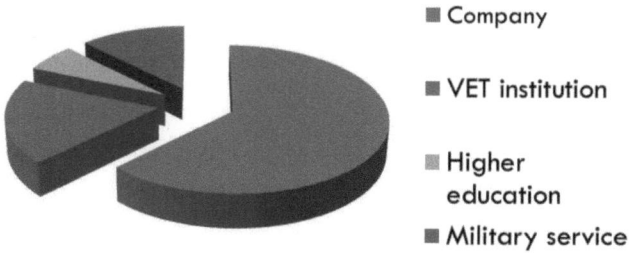

> There has been constant collaboration between the school and the company in order to ensure best correlation in theoretical and practical training. Also, the school trainers provided some advice regarding pedagogical aspects of training and shared their teaching experiences with the company staff.

> **Another important achievement is that in the new Labour Code of Lithuania, the draft of which has been proposed lately, apprenticeship (dual training) is recognized as a form of working contract. It can be considered as an essential step in facilitating and formalizing the work-based learning. During project life time, we had numerous meetings and consultations with the representatives from the Ministry of Science and Education during which we stressed the importance of this type of learning for Lithuanian VET.**

> Despite the successful piloting of the training model, some areas remain that need to be addressed and improved:

- *pedagogical training* for the company's staff,
- *longer duration* of the training programme,
- more *funding/support opportunities* from the state to the trainees and the company.

5.2. Implementation of the Hamburg Model in Hungary[25]

The school year began on September 1, 2014 with implementing previously developed training and realization programs. The school year was completed on 13.06.2015. This is followed by a summer internship that lasts 5 weeks (140 hours of practical lessons). This practical part started on 22.06.2015 and is completed end of July 2015.

Responsible for the general education and the specialized theoretical vocational training:

Tanext Academy Vocational School, Budapest

Trainer: Péter Daróczi

The practical vocatioal training was carried out in the enterprises Homo Novus Kft. & Motus and Talent Kft.. Both hold the necessary licence issued by the chamber to train students.

Instructors: László Nyitrai und Zsigmond Kéri

---

[25] The implementation report for Hungary is prepared by the implementing partner Laszlo Kajos and Istvan Mosoczi, Kontiki, June 2015, Budapest.

The program started with 16 participants who have chosen the occupations tiler/painter or decorator/bricklayer. 2 participants have left the Hamburg Model training by changing to a middle school, where they can achieve a high school graduation („Abitur"). The drop-out rate is considerably lower than in other educational programs. For all participants who have succesfully partcipated in the Hamburg Model, further professional training or professional activity is secured.

The training program had to ensure the integration into the training and the prevention of drop-outs through successful experiences for two different target groups.

1. <u>Part of the students was picked up after the 8th grade of general education in the Hamburg Model.</u> These students have participated together with other students in general education like communication (grammar and literature), mathematics, science, social sciences and English language, and also took part in the group activities of the students of the 9th grade.
Teachers for the general education: Edina Keller, Edina Antalfi, András Lázár

    The professional training of these students has begun with practical training in the construction industry. The participants received the for the practical part required theory by the trainers. After prior notice, the participants were allowed to swap parts of their general education classes in practical training. This was in the first half often the case. Despite this possibility, the students had to meet the requirements of general education, which all have made.

2. <u>The other part of the participants in the Hamburg Model were partly drop-out students from other schools; some of them were taken earlier in the Tanext Academy.</u> This group has not participated in general education respectively only partly to catch up lessons (reading, writing, arithmetic) in

small groups (2-3 people). The necessary general knowledge for a successful vocational training was tested in a special exam, the knowledge deficits can be made up.

The training subjects for the profession bricklayer were:
- Occupational health and safety,
- Activities in the construction industry,
- Bricklaying, plastering works,
- Concrete and ferroconcrete constructions.

The training subjets for the professions tiler/painter were:

- Occupational health and safety,
- Activities in the construction industry,
- Painter and decorator working,
- Painting on wood, on walls, on metal and on special areas,
- Decorators work

Within the Hamburg Model the priority was to provide sound training in the professional theory and practice.

The statutory competencies in the two professions are:

PERSONAL COMPETENCES:

Responsibility, compliance with rules, decision-making ability, punctuality, stereoscopic vision, motor skills, physical fitness, organizational skills, coordination of movements.

SOCIAL COMPETENCES

Leadership, acceptance of leadership, determination, helpfulness, willingness to match, feedback capability, contact capability, willingness to compromise, conflict resolution ability.

METHODOLOGICAL COMPETENCES

Systematization ability, diligence, caution, situational awareness, problem solving, troubleshooting, creativity, ingenuity, methodical work, practical task interpretation, systematic thinking.

As part of the Hamburg Model project also social skills such as self-knowledge, the ability to cooperate, conflict management were taught and developed by the participants. The activities of the S7 social services can be called successful.

Responsible for the development of social skills: Dr. Éva Győrfi, Szilvia Csató, Csilla foci.

Important experience of the first year was that the success in the practice has a direct link with the competencies developed during the Hamburg Model and had impact on the success of all other learning activities of the participants.

Time management within the Hamburg Model[26]
- 144 h general education,
- 180 h development of social competences,
- 72 h conflict management programs,
- 144 h profession related theory,
- 720 h practice,
- 140 h summer practice.

The success of the participants in the Hamburg Model was clearly identified due to the preponderance of practice.

The general education is assessed with scores of 1-5, which are supplemented with a written assessment and assessment of social skills.

The practical training will be evaluated by the professional instructors and approved by the school. In Hamburg Model there was not a single case where the school could have the review of the technical instructor not approved.

The average scores of the participants in the Hamburg Model were:
- General education: 2,57
- Profession related theory: 2,7
- Practice: 3,8

The Tanext Akademy Vocational School assess the Hamburg Model as very successful.

The education activities of the stuents were very positive.

The Tanext Academy has the Hamburg Model firmly established as a best practice in their training program and submitted to the authorities for approval. In the next

---

[26] Legal recommendation in Hungary 162 hours of profession related theory, 360 hours of practice, 140 hours Summer Practice, 648 hours of General Education.

school year, the recent professions and a new profession (social care) will be offered in the framework of the Hamburg Model.

The Hamburg Model and the experience gained in the practical implementation were intensively transferred to other vocational training providers and consulted with them. The consultations with the schools that are interested in the adaptation of the Hamburg Model in the next school year, were quite successful. Two schools have already informed bindingly that they will adapt the Hamburg Model in the next school year (Mándy vocational school, vocational school Pentelei Molnár). With more schools that are very interested in the discussions continue.

Likewise companies were informed about the Hamburg Model speficically and the dual vocational training generally. Some companies have already been involved in the training and further implementation of the Hamburg Model, such as Cemex Hungária Kft, Rékassy Glass Kft, Xella Hungária Kft.

More dissemination activities have been carried out on the Hamburg Model and the experiences of the pilot project, for example, via the newspaper "Modern Iskola", on TV channel of the districts Kőbánya and Kispest in Budapest, creation and dissemination of a summary of a study, and various presentations, for example: lecture on the "Hamburg Model" for directors of economic interest groups and micro enterprises of the V4 countries (Visegrad countries); Lecture on the "Hamburg Model" for the representatives of Hungarian teachers' associations; Consultations on the "Hamburg Model" with representatives of teachers' associations; Involvement in a professional educational cooperation with the Chamber of Bergamo (Italy) for the realization of the "Hamburg Model" program; presentations to representatives of the press; a conference on the experience gained and the adaptation possibilities of the "Hamburg Model" is carried out in Budapest in August 2015.

6. Evaluation of the piloting of the Hamburg Model in Lithuania and Hungary

Both trainings are evaluated by external evaluators: Gediminas Technical University in Vilnius and Corvinus University of Budapest. The evaluation methods and instruments are in both countries identical.

The evaluation was carried out in three steps: at he beginning in November 2014, in the middle in March 2015 and at the end of the training in June 2015 in bouth countries parallely.

The evaluation contains process and result evalution using a mix of methods from qualitative and quantitative empiric social research: guideline interviews (face-to-face interviews) and partly standardized questionnaire in order to examine as many aspects of the approach, subject and process as possible.

The target groups were: participants, lecturers and enterprises.

The summary of the evaluation results is given in the following chapter[27].

6.1. Evaluation results of the training in Lithuania[28]

The age structure of the trainees:

- 1 out of 16 trainees were female; 15 – male

---

[27] The whole and detailed evaluation reports can be found here: http://www.vet-bsr.eu/

[28] The complete evaluation and the evaluation report of the implementation of the Hamburg Model in Lithuania was prepared by habil. dr. prof. Romualdas Ginevičius, Vilnius Gediminas Technical University, Lithuania.

- The main group 50% of all 16 participating trainees was 18-19 years olds, followed by 19% of the participants in the age groups 20 – 21 and 24 – 25 and 12% aged 22 – 23.

Education background of the trainees:
- The most of the trainees have completed secundary education; almost half of them have already vocational school-leaving qualification in different occupations: tiler/plasterer, electrician, mechanics, waiter/bar man, car mechanic.

Previous experience of the trainees:
- 50% of all trainees were unemloyed between 1 – 16 months before the training.
- The half of the trainees were practising in other occupations before starting the training: autoelectrician, general construction works, painter, sales, warehouse keeper and worker protection.
- Almost 70% of all trainees were working on the construction site without required qualifications before; nearly 30% of them between 3 – 6 months.
- After completing the Hamburg Model training program 50% of all intend to work in the profession „Specialist for building insulation", 38% would like to continue the vocational training in the related occupation – decorator, 2 trainees would do something else.

Carrier plans in the next five years:
- 50% of all trainees do not have any plans reagarding their carrier
- 32% would like to be a good specialist in his occupational field
- 12% or 2 trainees out of 16 intend to find better job opportunities
- One trainee would like to have own company

The teacher profile:
- 60% of the school teachers involved in the program have a pedagogical education, 30 % - professional studies.

Aspiration for the future in the vocational education and training system by teachers:
- The vocational training should be fully conform with the EU standards
- The state should support financially the students (training allowance) and the enterprises
- There is a need to improve the vocational education and training system in Lithuania. The best way to do that is to introduce the dual education system

The profile of the entrprise:
- The profile of the company, where students had vocational training fully corresponded to the content of the considered programme, which was focused on the systems of facade heat insulation. This company has been working for fifteen years in the construction industry. It employs more than 60 workers and has been recently ranked to be among the best ten companies of this profile in Lithuania.

Summarising conclusions of the evaluation of the whole training **by company:**
- The manager of the company is responsible for the whole process of students training (organizing, supervision, instruction, etc.). However, it is

hardly fair. The responsible person with the respective qualification should to be appointed to this position under the order of director.

- The programme was evaluated very positively by the enterprise. On the one hand, it allowed students to consolidate the theoretical knowledge, to get the required professional skills because they performed all operations associated with wall insulation technologies. On the other hand, the company can train skilled workers for its own needs, to assess students' abilities, etc. The implementation of vocational training programmes should be based on law, with the expenses of vocational training in the company partially compensated under the law procedure. Now, the company, pays to students from their own funds.

- Vocational training in the company provides the conditions for supervising and training students so that they could become high quality workers and get the required assistance.

- The programme has an optimal relationship between theory and practice. It ensures the consistent and qualified application of theoretical knowledge to practical work because students have the possibility to spend more time in the company. It also provides another opportunity - the company can work closely, cooperate with the training centre and improve the content of the theoretical course.

- The company's responses show, that the content of the vocational training should be improved methodically within the company itself. This could be done in the following way: the whole training period should be divided into phases having their specific aims. These could be three phases, containing the preparation, as well as basic and final stages:
    - At the first stage, the aim is to acquaint the students with the work with technologies, tools, transactions, etc. Students should be taught how to use theoretical knowledge in performing specific operations.

- The aim of the second phase is the participation of students in the technological process, acquiring the required skills, etc.

- The aim of the third stage is the assessment of students' achievements.

During the piloting phase, all these tasks are done more intuitively.

- The company was highly satisfied with the students and their ability to apply theoretical knowledge in practice, while students were satisfied with the company and goodwill and kindness of their staff. Even 2/3 of the students would like to work in this company.

- Due to the successful vocational training, very close cooperation with the training centres has been established. The training centre can improve the theoretical part of the programme, while the company can improve the content of the vocational training.

- The company is interested in further cooperation with the training centre because in this case both parts win. It is necessary that the companies, together with training centres would rise questions about vocational training development at the national level, especially about the state support of these training programme.

- The company fully agrees that there should be more programmes in both number and variety in Lithuania.

by trainees:

- According to the answers of the trainees, the positive aspects of the considered vocational training programme are as follows: the possibility to work on the real construction site, the sufficiently long period of the training,

- the possibility to work as equal members, autonomous work and, most important, the possibility to draw wages.

- The equipment of the training centre and workshops cannot replace the real working conditions on the construction site, as well as building materials, equipment, technology and the organization of work.

- The success and results of practical training greatly depends on the instructor and his/her attitude towards the trainees and the ability to lead the vocational training.

- The theory is required when students want to become qualified workers. For example, the teachers of the training centre are able to explain better why in performing a specific operation, some particular materials should be used instead of other materials. The trainer in company often miss such knowledge. However, the practical work helps to understand the theory.

- The expectations regarding the training programme were met and even exceeded. Students were not expected to learn so many new things within a short period of time. They were not expected to draw wages.

- It is necessary that such type of the programme would be widely implemented in Lithuania. It would be very useful for students to have a possibility to work in different teams in order to compare the jobs and working conditions.

- Students will be also delighted to participate in such programme in the future. Such programs like Hambrug Model in dual system have to be as many and diverse as possible.

by teachers:

- Close cooperation between the teachers and the company is required. This cooperation should take place in the following way: teachers have to raise their qualification and closely cooperate with the company's employees responsible for practical training. In the training centre, theory and practice should be taught by the same teacher. In this case, working closely with the company he/she could improve the training.

- The cooperation between training centres and enterprises is particularly important during the training programme preparation. The working group should include representatives of both institutions – they have together to plan the programme, draw up the training plan for practical and theoretical training and schedule, etc. Teachers must attend students during practical training.

- The considered training programme provides many new opportunities for both training centres and well as the company. After performing practical training, students are aware of what theoretical knowledge they lack. The link between the training centres and companies is created, therefore, the theory and the content of practical training can be adjusted. Due to this cooperation, the training centre knows how to correct the content and consistency of vocational training, the requirements to future worker competences and skills.

- After performing the vocational training students become more interested in learning the theory. They better understand the theory, underlying new technologies, etc. Students become more motivated to become good professionals. Hence, the training program has proved its value.

- The time of the training programme was sufficient. It was enough time to satisfy the needs of learning. If the training programme were broader in content, the time would not be sufficient, because it is dedicated only to acquiring the primary skills. Therefore, in general it can be concluded that one-year is too short. The programme of vocational training should be 1,5 - 2 year long.

- Successful vocational training requires motivated students. This situation could be observed in this case, and therefore the scores of these students were higher than those of conventional curriculum students.

- An important result of the training programme implementation is that the most students expressed a wish to work for the certain company after the graduation. In order to have such a successful training, it is required that companies give more time for students' training, adaptation to the labour market, advertising specialities and professions, etc.

General conclusions

Conclusions of the first stage

- The number of school leavers coming to the vocational training centres has increased. Hence, the attractiveness of the vocational training has to be increased.

- The pedagogical qualification of vocational teaching staff has to be increased.

- The more effective vocational training forms such as the dual model implementaton are requested by enterprises.

Conclusions of the second stage

- Lithuanian vocational training centres have to be motivated to be the successful part in the dual model installation. It requires to solve following questions: its management, cooperation with the Lithuanian Confederation of Industrialists Builders Association, etc.

- The questions of the state participation in the process of the dual vocational training have to be solved (law, grants, etc.)

Conclusions of the third stage

- The implementation of the vocational programme shows that the period of one-year is too short. This question was raised by companies, leaders of training as well as trainees.
- In order to increase the effectiveness of the implementation of the dual training model, the qualification of teachers have to be raised, especially the pedagogical qualification.
- The companies have to be supported by the state financially to participate in the dual model implementation.
- The companies hesitate to introduce the Hamburg Model, because at the moment there are no favourable conditions for it in Lithuania: no tax benefits, no state funding; the financial and personnel, capacities of the companies do not allow to train trainees since the companies are very small; Moreover, the companies are afraid to allow trainees to work with sophisticated equipment.

Recommendations by the evaluator:

1. The capacities of the training centers/schools must be increased to implement such training programs.
    - At the moment, the teachers are afraid to loose their job by introducing the dual vocaional education.
    - The vocational schools lack on funding for modern equipment and materials, etc.

2. The capacities of the companies must be increased.

- To increase the motivation of companies to organise high-quality vocational training it is necessary to have financial supprt.

3. Laws and regulations should be reviewed and coordinated.

6.2. Evaluation results of the training in Hungary[29]

Evaluation phase I – at the beginning of the training

Questionnaires with the students, the enterprises and the lecturers

In the first evaluation the following target groups took part:

Distribution of participants	
Target group	Number of respondents
students	8
enterprises	3
lecturers	6

Thus, according to the numbers all participating lecturers and representatives of enterprises filled out the questionnaire but only a part of the students. The evaluator observed low motivation of students to answer the prepared questionnaires. Also it

---

[29] This book contains the summary of the evaluation results for Hungary; the complete evaluation and the evaluation report of the implementation of the Hamburg Model in Hungary was prepared by Dora Szegő, Corvinus University of Budapest and can be found here: www.vet-bsr.eu.

was hard for the teachers to motivate them filling out the questionnaires. A few of them did not provide valuable answers. It was much easier to motivate them during the interviews to provide answers. The interviews (the phase II) are the most valuable source of data about the students.

Nevertheless it is useful to summarise and present the summary of the results, which follow below.

Survey with the students

Basic information on the students

8 students completed the questionnaires. The average age of the students is 18,7 year. The youngest student is 17 years old, the oldest is 21. All of the respondents are male. Elementary school is the highest school degree for 6 of them, one of them has a completed vocational school degree in the construction sector, one of them a secondary technical school degree in the construction sector. 4 of them already started but haven't finished a vocational training as a bricklayer, cook and computer technician. 2 of the respondents have been working in the construction sector for more than one year, although they have a vocational degree in other profession, not related to the construction sector. One of them worked in other jobs before the training started. None of the respondents was unemployed before the training, most of them were students, and the rest of them were working.

Professional goals in the next future
- 6 of them reported that they want to work in the profession that they study
- two of them wanted to do further professional training in another profession

In the next 5 years

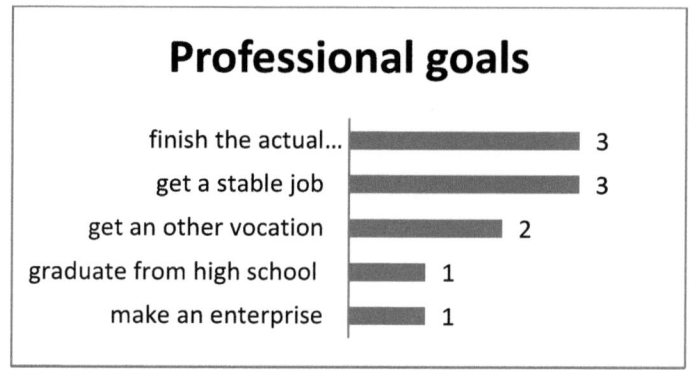

Evaluation of the training

After the first few month of the theoretical training student opinions were quite divided about the theoretical part. However, the majority, 75% of them found the aims of the theoretical training rather clear. Students felt less prepared for the practice after theoretical classes: only 37,5% of them found himself absolutely prepared, 37,5% of them rather or strongly disagreed with that statement.

50% of the respondents strongly or rather agreed that the lecturer could convey the content well, 25% rather or strongly disagreed with that.

50% of them saw an overlap between the knowledge at theory and practice, 37,5% of them perceived a lack of an overlap between the two. 62,5% of them found that the knowledge gained in theory classes is well-applicable in practice, and 25% rather or strongly disagreed with that. Finally, the majority, 62,5% of the respondents found the scope of theory lessons satisfactory.

After the first impressions of the practical training, all respondents agreed that they would need more assistance in practice. The training at least rather met the expectations of 75% of the respondents; only one student was rather dissatisfied. 87,5% was pleased with the training so far, and the same amount of them would rec-recommend the company to their friends for training. 75%-of the respondents rather or strongly agreed that they do something productive for the company, only one student disagreed. 75% of them hope that they can work for the company after the training, only one of them has strong concerns against that. The majority of the students perceived the instructors as pedagogically well-prepared, although one of them strongly disagreed with that. 87,5% of them thought that they had enough time to get an insight into all areas of activities in the company, one student rather disagreed with that. 67,5% perceived that they are fully involved in the operational process, 25% rather or strongly disagreed with that. Most of the students were satisfied with the premises, equipment and facilities of the practical training only one of them expressed dissatisfaction about that. Most of the students evaluated the working atmosphere positively, and found the aims of the practical training clear. 67,5% of the students found that the instructor takes enough time to explain the work tasks, 25% of the students rather or strongly disagreed with that statement. Most students found the working part at the company useful, the scope of practice satisfactory and the idea of more practice than theory useful.

Survey with the enterprises

Basic information on the enterprises

All the enterprises involved in the dual system of vocational training at Kontiki are small enterprises; the number of employees is between 8-17. The economic sector is construction industry. In all companies there is an assigned person who takes responsibility of the training (instructor). In all cases they are the respondents of the questionnaires. In most of the companies the responsible person is an employee of the company, a managing/senior skilled worker. Two of the instructors have a pedagogical qualification as trainers. One of them has a vocational certification in the profession.

Motivation of the companies to participate in the program

The most popular motivation behind the participation in the training program among the companies was the desire to help to integrate young people and the aim to support the realization of practical training in companies. One instructor preferred to get qualified personnel in this way. They haven't seen that the dual system of vocational training would be the channel for the company to gain appropriate professionals or specialists and none of them mentioned the inefficiency of a sole-school education among their reasons to support the Hamburg model training.

Opinion about financial support and funding

All instructors agreed that for the implementation of this training within the company the state should support the company financially, and the company should support the student as well. Opinions were divided about the appropriate amount of the monthly state support between 40.000 HUF / 130 EUR per student and 10.0000 HUF / 320 EUR per student. There was a wider consensus on the financial education allowance for the students, which should be a form of 'scholarship' according to the instructors, with the amount of 30-40.000 HUF /100- 130 EUR monthly. **They also perceived the need for a wider support of the state with offering practical training centres and giving a discount on tools, on equipment and on material for the schools.**

Assessment of the Hamburg Model

When asking about the assessment of the one year long Hamburg Model training at the beginning of the training period, there was a wide consensus among instructors in most questions:
- All participants strongly agreed or rather agreed that the ratio of practice and theory is appropriate.

- The information exchange between the theoretical teachers at school and the instructors at the company is an essential condition for the good quality of the training.
- All respondents strongly agreed that the companies and the practical trainers should be more involved in the formation of the structure, the curriculum and the requirements of the training.
- There was a broad consensus on the issue that theory learned in school can be well-applied in the practical training and that the vocational training fits well in their enterprise.
- All agreed that the students are well-suitable for the Hamburg Model.
- The aims of the training are clear for all.
- They all agreed that participants are fully integrated in the operating process in the company and that the students get an insight into all areas of activity in the company.
- All of the instructors found their pedagogical education level appropriate for the task of instructing and supervising the students.
- All of them at least rather agreed that the company wants to employ a participant/participants after completing the training in their company.
- There was a wide consensus that the students contribute productively to the company already during the training.
- They would recommend other companies to participate in this professional training and were all in all very pleased with the training so far, which met their expectations.
- The most instructors see the length of the theoretical and practical part equally too short. They would extend the whole time period of the training, one of the three instructors assess the length of the training appropriate.

Survey with the lecturers

Basic information on the lecturers

6 lecturers who teach the Hamburg model students completed the questionnaire. We can consider them as experienced lecturers, since the average length of their

working practice in vocational education is 5 year. All of them are full-time employ-employees. 4 of them graduated from pedagogical college, two of them gained a vocational degree and a high school degree. One of them has a practical work experience in a company.

Opinion about financial support and funding

75% of the lecturers agreed that the state should financially support those companies who participate in the education program. The amount of preferred support varied between 50000-100000 HUF / 160- 320 EURO per student. 25% of the lecturers rather preferred the option of a financial education allowance for the students instead of the companies. Four lecturers supported the idea of a financial education allowance for students supplementary to the company support. They appointed the optimal amount of the student support between 10000- 30000 HUF / 30 -100 EUR per student. When talking about additional forms of support one of the respondents mentioned the **support with equipment and tools**. An additional idea was **a 'success award'** if a student graduates from vocational training. That could raise students' motivation further.

Opinion about the dual system of vocational training

83% of the respondents emphasized that the dual system of vocational training helps the integration of the youth in the vocational education and on the labour market, 50% of the lecturers mentioned that it is a very good model, 50% of them highlighted that it is better than pure classroom training, 50% of them agreed that it should be applied especially for young people with learning difficulties, 33% mentioned that it allows a better focus on the needs of the labour market.

Ideas, plans for the future in vocational training

Concerning the ideas, plans for the future about vocational education, lecturers mentioned that the companies have an interest in training skilful students for the company. Thereby it would be required that they put financial and other resources into the education. Some lecturers argued that the legislation should be changed to offer a sufficient framework for the dual training. E.g.: companies should be bound by regulation to employ students.

Assessment of the first year of the training model

Five of the lecturers agreed that theory and practice are well-connected in this training. One of them strongly disagreed with that statement. He was the one, who formulated the opinion that the practical training should follow more the theoretical curriculum, and perceived a significant gap between the timing of the two. From a lecturer's perspective it was a disadvantage of the practical training that it does not cover the theoretical curriculum. Although the interviews highlighted some other aspects of the working practice that explained the diversion of the timing (see the Report on Phase II.)

There was a full consensus among the theoretical lecturers that the exchange with the enterprises is good and the practically learned knowledge can be well applied in the theoretical training.

Four teachers strongly or rather agreed that the participants bring in the lessons experiences gained in the enterprises, one of them rather disagreed, one of them did not answer to that question.

There was a wide consensus that the students will be predominantly employed in the company after completing the vocational education, only one of them had doubts about that. All teachers considered the students' work during the training productive for the company. All of them would recommend other schools to implement such vocational training.

Evaluation phase II – in the middle of the training - Face-to-Face interviews with the trainees, lecturers and instructors

Interviews with the trainees

Evaluation of the training in general

We conducted all together 3 interviews with trainees who participate in two vocational courses: bricklayer-tiler and painter.

All Hamburg model students work for the company who does the reconstruction of a storage building called 'ATTraktár' and of the main school building. The storage building used to be a hangar of an enterprise. Right now it is under construction, and they complete it for the purposes of the vocational courses: they build vocational training rooms and workshops for the students and a rehearsal room and stage for the artiste students. The vocational students are **intensively involved in the construction works** of the venue. Besides that they do **reconstruction work in the school building, such as painting walls, masonry**. Later on (typically in second year) students accompany the instructor to other working sites as well:

'When I will be upper year student, I can go with the trainer to paint a real house. As a first year student I reconstruct the building of the vocational training facilities – that is real work too.' (painter student)

All of the interviewees are first year vocational school students participating in the Hamburg Model program. Unlike in other, conventional vocational trainings they are working **together at the company with second and third year students** of the same profession. The Hamburg Model students considered that structure as a **positive feature of the training**, because they could **ask for help** from the more educated students who answer their questions and **assist them** to do their task properly. On the other hand they **get a wider insight into the working procedure** than if they studied separately. Sometimes they even experimented with more complicated tasks during the year:

'If I don't know something, older students tell it. It is very good that we learn together with them. They help us how to do this, how to do that. I even tried a senior task once, glazing and wallpapering. The students showed me how to do it.' (painter student)

They mentioned **plastering, cleaning surfaces, preparing surfaces, using the ladder, securing the fellow-worker on the ladder –as main tasks** that they realized at the company during the year:

'sometimes we have to walk with the ladder on 10 m high pillars. We have to bring down the iron tubes. Two of us work in the heights at the same time. One of us is holding the ladder, the other one has the hammer – 5 kg, and the bricklayers have to prepare the surface for whitewashing'.

Students emphasized a further positive aspect of the Hamburg Model-based vocational training at Tannest school: students studying a profession in the construction industry can **get an insight into the other building industry professions**. They are going to be more skilled that way. Moreover there is **flexibility across the different training courses**. If a student does not like a vocation he/she can switch to another one during the training. Such flexibility does not exist in the conventional vocational training system of Hungary.

All of the interviewees finished elementary school and continued directly after that in the Kotaik vocational school department. One of them went to an elementary school for children with special needs. When reporting about the school choice, they told that they could find open places to apply for much later than in other schools. Some of the students missed all other application procedures due to family problems or moving to a different city. It was a big advantage for them that they could still apply for an admission into Kotaik at the end of the summer, when other school applications were already closed. In comparison with the elementary school they preferred Kotaik. They highlighted the humanistic approach towards students and the great amount of care. For example one of the students was a victim of bullying in his former school environment. He emphasized that such things could never happen in Kotaik, because the school makes efforts against it. The students referred to the social workers and the restorative circles that aim to solve conflicts with dialogues and to create a school climate where students feel safe:

'This is a better school than the one I attended before. I mean friendships. Many kids hated me in the elementary school. Some of them bullied me. It could never happen here. The school doesn't let them to do that. We even saw a video what they do with kids who do that. People talk things through and reconcile people. Not like in elementary school that you are being stood in the corner if you made something wrong' (painter student)

When asking them about deficiencies of the training, all of them mentioned the **scholarship as a possible motivating factor** that they haven't received yet. The state public administration is responsible for that delay- according to their best knowledge. Although they told that the school offered the possibility of a prepayment if a student is in need. Some of them told that they *'did not want to ask for prepayment, because the school has to prepay it and we do not want to punish the school because of the state's failure'*.

Choosing the school and the profession

Main motives behind the school choice were the **lack of tuition fee**, the **location of the school** – that it is not far and that it is not in a disreputable neighborhood and **'demanded professions' available on the course list**. An important positive aspect, what students highlighted concerning the entrance exam that *'the teachers were not interested in what I know from the curriculum but how I am as a person'*. For most of the students the **vocation was not a sufficiently informed and conscious career choice.** They wanted to choose a vocation in the building industry but the **limits of the supply of vocations determined the decision.**

Information and awareness-raising were those areas of the training where students articulated the **need for improvement**. They **did not get enough information** about the profession itself: what it means to be a bricklayer or a painter in practice. They formulated the need for **strengthening the career and study orientation by awareness raising conversations and a visit to the constructions**. These would be very useful and help students to make a sufficient decision about the vocation choice. That opinion was reinforced by the instructors from the enterprises as well (see in chapter II.).

Evaluation of the support and supervision in the company

Students **evaluated the amount of support and supervision in the practice positively. One assigned person is responsible for the students in each vocation, but the two instructors are assisting each other** – sometimes the bricklayer instructor supervises the group of the painters and vice versa. **Both instructors are skilled in both professions** and can assign tasks and supervise tasks equally. They are responsible for all together about 10 bricklayer and 6 painter students, although each student (including the Hamburg model students) have a different schedule coming to the construction. In the students view **the number of students at one time is ideal**. The instructors are not very overloaded, although one student mentions that a bit more attention to the students would be favorable. Students highlighted the **professionalism, good explanatory skills and patience of the instructors. Personal relationship** between the students and the instructors is of great importance. Some students told that the main motivation for them to come to the practice was that they didn't want to disappoint the instructor; they wanted to match his expectations.

One of the students mentioned that the instructors **should be 'more strict' with the demotivated students** who do not come to work regularly. Some students did not come to practice or are destructive when they are present - he finds it demotivat- demotivating for the work ethic of the whole group:

'Some students say I won't go there to mess up myself. That how their attitude is. And if they come once in a while, it is even worse. It happened once that they intentionally ruined the wall that we fixed, another time they kicked everything apart. They are destructive'.

The students also mentioned that the instructors at the enterprise **made several efforts to motivate the absent students.** E.g. they even hold a class about work ethic and about the perspectives if they drop out of school: *'they told us what perspectives are open for us if we do not finish any school and we do not get a profession. You can be either a garbage man or a homeless. Everyone participated on that. But it did not have any impact. The same people came to work on the following day and the same people stay away'. (bricklayer student)*

Students articulated the need for **more advice and counseling about entering the job market and job seeking.** Although – in the opinion of the teachers and instructors – it is part of the education, but not the task of the first year. I find it yet promising that first year students are already aware of that need. Most students interviewed want to find a job in the profession they study now, although their plans for the future are not very clear and well-elaborated yet.

Additional practice-related difficulties mentioned by the students were the cold temperature in the constructions during the winter, and the **'unsuitability' of some students for the chosen profession.** E.g.: some painter students are afraid of heights, which make cooperation with each other more difficult:

'Everything is good in the practical training. Except when I have to go up to the pillars with a fellow- student who is afraid of heights. We are always so worried for them and if they fall down from the heights.' (painter student).

Link between theoretical and practical units

Students **started practical education a few months after the start of the first semester.** The practical and theoretical training takes place on specific days of the week. **Students preferred the dominance of practice**, according to their opinion **the ratio of theory and practice is sufficient**. In their interpretation there is **a lack of connection between the theoretical and practical training**. They find it difficult to understand 'pure theory ' - described in the books. They would find it **easier to learn theory if it was more connected to practice**. Sometimes they lack the practical aspects of theory, the illustration of the equipment and material.

'In my opinion what we study in theory we should try it out in practice, demonstrating it with the equipment and tools - it would help understanding a lot' (bricklayer student)

The conditions of the building that the students build determine the working phases: students are **allowed to practice those working phases of painting and bricklaying what is needed in the building**. E.g.: *'we cannot practice flooring yet, because there is no surface to floor at the moment'. (bricklayer student)* The students' opinion about that condition is ambivalent. On one hand they find it **more difficult to link theory and practice due to the gap between the structure of the theoretical curriculum and the real needs of work** in the building. But on the other hand they **find it more realistic** that the way how they learn **practice is closer to a real construction procedure** than if it mechanically followed the theoretical curriculum.

They raise the idea of making practical and theoretical education at the venue of the constructions: **the theoretical part should be integrated into practice** - if that happened the teachers could illustrate more theory with the tools. Some efforts were made on that. The instructors established a 'lecture-corner' in the building that is under construction, where they often **demonstrated some theory for the working processes before the students started to do it in practice**. The students found that **very useful and well-functioning**.

Expectations and goals from the training

Students **did not have clear expectations** from the training. They were rather looking for guidance from the instructors and the teachers. They were mostly accustomed to failure, and lack of an experience about **acceptance, enough time and space for studying and allowance of making mistakes** in their previous education path. These were those features of the first year of the Hamburg model-based education that students really **appreciated** and that can be considered as a **retain capacity of the students** for the next year.

Would you participate in the program again? Would you recommend participating to others?

All the interviewees would choose the same school again, and the same program, although they would prefer an **extension of the offer of the construction industry professions** in the school. They would be motivated to join another profession in the building industry.

Interviews with the representatives of the enterprises

We conducted **two interviews with the representatives of two enterprises**, who are **responsible for the practical training and instruction of the Hamburg model students in bricklaying-tiling and painting**. The interviews **covered the total number of instructors** in the program. Both companies work on the reconstruction of the building of 'ATT-raktár', and the main school building. Final year students also accompany the instructors to other working sites. Both enterprises are **small enterprises with 8-17 employees**.

Involvement of the students into the operational process

There are about ten students in each profession. Hamburg Model students study together with the rest of the students (2nd and 3rd year students); they have a different weekly time schedule. About **4 students work at the same time** by each company. The students **work with a vocational training contract**. The bricklayer instructor's opinion matched the students that **working together with upper year students is an advantage**. Although they got different tasks, older students helped the first year students. Answering the question 'what kind of work the students do at the company' – the bricklayer instructor said: *'everything from A to Z.* **Masonry, concrete work, everything that a bricklayer-tiler has to do**. *And, what is important. Not like traditional teaching that I show it once. I show it 30 times and finally they get it.'*

There were a few students who have (minor) mental disability. It is very difficult to make them understanding the processes. The instructor has to show it many times until it is settled. Both companies did reconstruction work in buildings used by the Kontiki school. They reconstructed the building that hosts the educational facilities (workshops, storages, rehearsal room for the artistes) of the practical training. It means that they did **real work** for the labor market but in a *'**safe environment**'* – as the bricklayer instructor phrased. In his opinion it is an important element of the dual vocational training. The students experienced that they build something that is going to be used. Sometimes they boasted about it that *'I did that concrete surface over there'*.

Upper year students already accompany the instructors to other constructions as well. In those situations **when they work for other clients not the school most of the work is done by the instructor, but the students assist him**: *'they cut material, they give the equipment, and they measure' (bricklayer instructor)*. The bricklayer instructor found it very important that the students have to be put to *'deep water'*, where they perceive that they have to **match expectations** and demonstrate their knowledge. But this has to be made **gradually**. First **they work in the reconstructions of the school**, where *'they know that I am, - as instructor - responsible for what they do. If you bring first year students to a client they will fail. But if you strengthen them in the safe environment where it is allowed to make mistakes, they will already know what to do when they get to other clients. You should not protect them of these experiences, because wherever they go they will meet expectations...'*

Furthermore when more students work together at one company it is a *'**demo for a work organization**. Students take roles. Some are skillful in certain things, others in other* *things. They share the work based on their skills and capabilities. That's how it is going to be at the real workplace as well*.

Getting used to work on the school buildings was in accordance with the clients' needs as well, who – in the opinion of an instructor – do not want to teach students. Clients need students for work. If 2-3 absolutely inexperienced students go to a client, then those students are rather a burden for the company who wants the work to be accomplished. Second year students who already have some work experience and routine in a secure working environment can be useful in a less safe working environment as well.

The painting instructor highlighted another aspect of the same question: *'you have to teach them gradually. The point is not to drop them into the deep water but rather accommodate them slowly. The point of the training is not that the students get to a workplace, but first that they get used to work, develop passion for the profession.'*

Students' motivation and integration to the labor market

In the instructors opinion both the painter and the bricklayer-tiler profession are difficult, because the labor market opportunities are uncertain. But these professions are demanded in the labor market.

These students are **disadvantaged** with those parts of the professions that **require counting**. However, according to their opinion these **disadvantages can be bridged during the dual vocational training**. They placed an emphasis to the **motivation of the students.** *'Who takes the training seriously will find a job'*- as they say. The instructors emphasized that **many students do not have a 'real motivation'** towards the profession chosen. They are not interested in it. They come to the course because the parents force that they should learn a profession, or because they feel good in the company of other students. According to the opinion of the instructors, **about the half of the Hamburg model students are motivated**, the other half is *'only drifting'*. Although one of the instructors mentioned that counter examples also exist and **it is possible to make** originally **demotivated students motivated** with the proper pedagogical means: *'It happens that someone is drifting for a year and suddenly he realizes the importance of the profession and starts to work'.*

When asking about the means for motivating, instructors said it is very important that the **student has to *'believe that they know what they get to know'.*** These students usually have a very low self-esteem and don't believe that they gain what they get to learn. *'He is very skillful and knows something but he still claims that he doesn't know.'*- That negative self-esteem is fed by the previous negative educational experiences. It can be a **serious obstacle of learning and burden of motivation**. Students are not motivated to try out a difficult task, e.g: cutting YTONG Blocks because they anticipate failure. These **situations can be turning points** where the instructors have to help and facilitate a situation where the **student gets an experience that he can do it**. Bad experiences and patterns can be overwritten very slowly by time and gain a lot of patience.

The painter instructor would put **higher emphasis on learning a foreign language**. Knowing English or German language opens the labor market chances towards the neighboring countries and **significantly raises the chances of getting a job**.

Assistance of professional orientation

Instructors also highlighted the **importance of awareness-raising at the beginning of the training**. The lack of a conscious career choice was affirmed by the fact that only about one third of the first year students who started the training participated regularly on the courses. The two third of them left the classes when they realized what bricklaying or paining means in practice. A few of them were not well suited for these professions - either their 'body condition' or their personality did not make them suitable for the profession according to the instructors.

General evaluation of the program

The instructors agreed that the **early start and the overweight of practical education is a good model**, because these students are **much more receptive for practice than for theory**. The main obstacle concerning the practical training is the **motivation and readiness of students to be present at work**.

Evaluation of the supervision

The instructors confirmed that one, assigned instructor is responsible for the students. As the bricklayer instructor phrased, '*the* **system and order of work has to be well-elaborated and followed***. The main point is that when the student arrives, he has to know what his task is: there are phases that* **have to be automatisms***, like washing the equipment, cleaning the venue – these have to be routinized.*'

The other important aspect of supervision stressed by the instructors was the **clear assignment of tasks**. Tasks have to be assigned previously: students have to know what their task is on the next day. The instructors confirmed what some students also mentioned that keeping discipline is an area that could be improved:

'*Some slight changes are needed concerning discipline. If we work, then we work. Flexibility is not allowed there. If we work, or if I explain the tasks, working atmosphere should approach the standards of a real working environment. Nobody is allowed to chat about off-topics*'.

A further aspect of supervision that was mentioned is the **personal relationship** between the instructor and the students. Most students come from difficult family environment. Principally the social workers accompany the education process and take care for the students' mental health. But in some cases the **students choose the instructor as a 'trusted person'**. Instructors thought that they have to **accept that**

role to a certain degree. That was **part of their task as instructors, including the consultation with the social workers** about the students. The social workers also helped the instructors to achieve the students' presence on practical lessons.

As the painter instructor said: *'they can improve in our personal relationship. I am sometimes a substitute father for them. I take that role although it is important to keep the three step distance'*- he also spoke about the **difficulty of keeping the emotional distance** and boundaries as instructors.

Link between theory and practice

The instructors emphasized that the **conditions of the practical education facility determine the curriculum of the practical training: they can practice only those tasks that match the needs of the construction: concrete work, masonry, plastering,** - they do what is just needed on the site. **They have a limited scope on that. It is consistent with the learning curriculum** in their opinion but **it requires a different learning structure than 'textbook version'**. From the instructors perspective **it is not a deficiency, rather an advantage, because the students can see how a construction process is built up in a 'real-life situation'**. They see all working processes. Nothing is left out but they **get to know it in a structure that is different from the theoretical scenario**. The topics are also different in theory and in practice: operation order, materials, health and safety are issues of theoretical classes. Practice is more focused on technics and the usage of the tools.

On the school's initiative a **conscious effort was made** by instructors and lecturers **to harmonize theory and practice**. The instructors and the theoretical lecturers negotiated about the curriculum. The theoretical lecturer came to the construction for a visit. But as the bricklayer instructor mentioned **it was difficult to give constructive advices for each other**. The theoretical lecturer **is used to the traditional educational system**, where he is responsible for his own subject. They gave advices and feedbacks very reluctantly for each other, because they did not want to challenge the other teacher's competence. Nevertheless, the main area that should be harmonized according to the instructor is **the 'language use'**. Sometimes it happened that the students got confused, when they used different terms for the same tasks/objects in theory and in practice. Furthermore instructors agreed that steps have to be made within reasonable boundaries **to approach the timing of topics in theory and practice.**

An additional negative circumstance regarding the link between theory and practice was that many students **only attended the practical courses and hardly participated on the theoretical lessons.** There were some students who **always came to the practice, even instead of the theoretical class**. The instructors tried to make it clear that it is useless that way, because they won't get a degree without theory. The bricklayer instructor even accompanied a student to the theoretical lesson, but on the next day he came to practice instead of theory again. In the instructors' opinion **these students underline the legitimacy of the Hamburg Model and show how determining the students' practical orientation is**. It would be a mistake to lose those students who do not attend the theoretical lessons. According to the instructors an optimal construction would be **to integrate the theory into practice and make the theoretical education in the practical facilities**. They already have an experience about that scenario: when one of the instructors substituted the theoretical lecturer he made the theory class on the construction. They **established a classroom with a blackboard** and he demonstrated the theoretical lesson with the help of the equipment and material, which was *'very handy'*. This seemed to be very effective and well- for the students.

Goals of the training and their clarity

One instructor mentioned that although the students had an idea about the training **but did not see through the whole learning procedure**, which is a

deficiency, because most students did not know what a bricklayer or painter job consists of. They **realized that it did not match their expectations only when facing the working procedure**:

'The new fellows thought that they want to be bricklayers, but they did not have a clue what it means. When they started, some of them could handle it. Others started to realize that they do not want to be messy every day. They do not want to pack and clean every day, etc. I told them that if you will be a bricklayer-tiler, that will be your job for your whole life. You have to tell them at the very beginning: you will shovel, you will do concrete work, you will do masonry. It works like that every day. You should not complain every day. You have to like at least to a certain degree what you do. If you cannot like it, you should not do it.'

– in his opinion these **questions should be clarified in the very beginning, before a student chooses a profession**. He has to be 'introduced' into a day of a bricklayer and the working process. **Kontiki is more flexible than other schools** from the point that students can switch to another profession if they realize that they do not match.

Expectations about the students and the school

The instructors said that if they had to decide it now, **they would join the training program again.** As a main expectation they want to reach that **all students are present both on the practical and theoretical classes**. They would like to make the students **well-prepared to the final exam and compensate their disadvantages to make them suitable for the labor market.** Their expectations from the school are to 1. give more information about the professions to the students and put extra efforts into awareness-raising and 2. support the students' presence with all available resources.

Interviews with the lecturers

We conducted three interviews with teachers. One of them was the theoretical lecturer of painters and teaches construction fundamentals, environment, health and safety subjects since 2014, the other ones were a social worker, responsible for competence development (among other tasks) and an English teacher – both of them has been teaching in the school for four years.

General evaluation of the program

The social worker mentioned the students' attitude as a key topic that determines the success of the program, the theoretical lecturer **put the focus on the gap between the theoretical and practical education**: *'Theory has a specific scenario. The students perceived it as a problem that they did not know a topic in theory but they already have to do it in practice. I tried to calm them down that by the end of the training it will all come together. It is very difficult to make them understand'.*

In their opinion the **selected professions** of the Hamburg Model in Hungary are **good choices**. Bricklayer-tiler and painter are professions were skilled labor force is needed. Foreign working opportunities are also open. But there is a great selection of professionals. **Only those professionals are needed who are 'well-skilled'**. Gaining a paper is not enough in itself. That's an additional circumstance why motivation is very essential. The lack of motivation is a great deficiency of the students of the school. Very few of them is ready to learn. The theoretical lecturer does not believe in liberal atmosphere when working with that group of students, because they do not appreciate partnership. **He considered the vocational training contract a very good idea if the school complies with it. It has to be monitored and kept much more serious** in his opinion. A further motivating factor is **the scholarship for the students. Creating a framework,** 'run the game' within that framework and **keep the boundaries** are the most important factors that could initiate a change in students' attitudes in the opinion of the English teacher. As an example, the theoretical lecturer mentioned the need for **being strict about late**

arrivals. At the beginning the students arrived at 11 am to morning classes instead of 9. The theoretical lecturer achieved that now those who arrive come in time.

'Personal tone and being open for their interest is also a tool for building trust and make them cooperative. When they are very disoriented in the class I initiate a conversation about their own topics like alcohol, girls, parties and they become motivated. We need to build the professional issues of the lecture around these topics to make them present.' – as the theoretical lecturer phrased.

Additional resources for the teachers are the **few motivated and cooperative students who can function as *'pull factors'* for the others. Teaching methods are very different with the students of this program than in other schools.** Most students are 'functionally illiterates' – they have inadequate reading and writing skills. The lecturers had to **simplify the curriculum and make it very 'pure'**. To match the students capabilities they **did not use the textbook much, rather the lecturer's note** that contained the 'thick description' of the textbook with only those terminologies that were necessary. They tried to **build more on conversation than on reading and writing.**

Link between theory and practice

The theoretical lecturer agreed that **more practice is needed than theory. He found the emphasis of practical education a good model. He also agreed to start practice at the beginning.**

The opinion of the theoretical lecturer about harmonizing the curriculum of theory and practice was more negative than the instructors': **theory and practice could not be harmonized because the practice is bond by the given conditions of the constructions. Developing theory and practice in parallel is not a realistic expectation.** Students do completely different task than in theory. Otherwise, **the theoretical training could benefit a lot from what students already learned in practice,** students use their practical knowledge in theory lessons. For most of them theory is very difficult without practice – **practice is a great aid for them**, it is much easier to understand theory when they already tried out a task in practice.

The evaluation of the **exchange between school and company is positive**. The theoretical lecturer said that both the instructor and the lecturer **knew how the other is proceeding with the curriculum. They shared information with each other.**

Choosing the school and the profession

Just like the instructors, the lecturer and the teachers thought that **the students choose the profession rather '*accidentally*' than consciously**. Students don't see the '*dark sides of a profession*' – **they have an idealized picture of the professions** in construction industry:

'It shows a lot that when I asked them none of the students mentioned that he wants to be a bricklayer or a painter. They want plenty of other things to learn or do that are not realistic scenarios.' (Theory lecturer)

For many of the students the school is the only medium for socialization:

'Even if the students live in a family it seems to be like if they were living alone. They don't speak about the parents at all.' (Theory lecturer)

- the family does not provide a structure and regularity in their lives. The school has a very difficult task if it does not match with the families expectations. E.g.: the question of punctuality with time exemplifies that dilemma. Students arrive to the classes and to the construction often at 11 am, which is unacceptable in the realm of construction industry.

The sufficiency of school units to meet the learning needs

The lecturer mentioned the **lack of appropriate amount of equipment and tools** in theoretical education. Sometimes he brought his own equipment for demonstration to help understanding – it was **much easier for the students to understand things when they saw** it. He also told that the school was **developing the equipment supply continuously**. The instructors' idea to **integrate the theory into practice** and make the theoretical education in the practical facilities **could be a solution for the supply of equipment as well**:

'Buying more equipment (e.g.: for the decoration painting) would be a great financial investment, but it would be necessary to make the theoretical training more useful. The students could hold the tools in their hands and try out how to use them. Many times they learn it in paper, but when they meet the equipment on the construction they don't know what it is. They cannot recall it from their theoretical studies, because they did not try it out on the theory lesson – it is a big mistake I think.' (Theory lecturer)

They felt more need for **visual tools for demonstration,** since these students are **more receptive for visual experience than for verbal**. E.g.: **videos of the working process** or about **the demonstration of equipment and material** – e.g.: alums, coloring matters. Especially the chemical processes could be demonstrated much more effectively via visuality. The lecturer mentioned that these videos are very expensive. He hoped that the international partnership might provide some opportunities in that respect (e.g.: **subtitling videos that are available in the model program of other countries**).

A further aspect that would assist the theoretical training would be **physical stability of the training rooms**. The size of the school building and the structure of the various educational units did not make it possible to **have a fixed room** for the theoretical lessons. They had to go here and there. For that special group of students **stability would be an aid to take it more seriously and assist presence on the classes.**

The theoretical lecturer became uncertain from time to time if it worth to continue teaching with these group of students or not. If he had to decide it now, he would not join the training program again. On one hand it was a great challenge but **the**

ratio of failures is much higher and he **experienced a very few obvious results**. Sometimes it felt hopeless to raise willingness to learn. The school could **help effi-efficiency with being stricter with the vocational training contract** and **make it compulsory for the students to be present on the classes and sanctioning** the absences.

SWOT analysis based on the interviews

Strengths	Weaknesses
the training is flexible for individual needs (e.g.: opportunity to switch for another profession during the training period)	some students lack motivation and do not visit the classes regularly (especially theory)
dominance of practice the ratio of theory and practice is sufficient students are receptive for practice	students lack information about the profession at the beginning of the training
there are ‚real' working conditions on the constructions	The choice of the profession is not conscious and thorough
students participate fully in construction work: there is an opportunity to try out all working phases in practice	lack of correspondence in the structure, timing and language use of theory and practice
the working contract	some equipment on the theoretical

	lectures are missing
students work together with more skilled, upper year students	the venue of the theoretical lectures is changing (due to the high number of students and the limits of the building)
the working environment is secure	
there is a good exchange and relationship between instructors and theoretical lecturers	
personal relationship between the instructors and the students inspire the students	
the instructors and lecturers are flexible and motivated. Ready to improve the training further	
Opportunities	**Threats**
strengthening the career and study orientation by awareness raising and informing at the beginning	the professions chosen are not suitable for some students
conversations about career choice and visits to the constructions	
to be more strict and consistent about frameworks	some students drop out
to monitor the working contract and comply with it	

to integrate theory into practical education (do theory lessons on the practical working facility)	
develop the equipment supply of the theoretical lectures further	demotivated students get the certificate without a proper/ thorough knowledge of the profession
methodological development, using more visual material in theory. e.g.: videos	
to offer more profession choices in the construction industry	

Evaluation part III – at the end of the training

Questionnaires with the students, enterprises and teachers

Survey with the students
- Based on the willingness of attending the classes and fulfilling the questionnaires it can be concluded that those students who were motivated during the first training year were rather the younger students. Elementary school is the highest school degree for all of them; none of them has a completed vocational school degree. For three of them the present training is the first vocational course they've started. Two of them started a previous vocational training before but they quit. Their age, the lack of professional experience and the hope for getting the first vocational degree can be motivating factors for attending the bricklayer-tiler or painter classes.
- It is remarkable compared to the first round of questionnaires that while in the first round many students wanted to get a degree in another profession (not the one they are studying now) – in the second round of questionnaires

they have not articulated that intention. On the contrary, **all of them rein-reinforced that they want to work in the profession that they have been studying** Asking for the individual carrier goals: *'get the degree and be able to work in the profession'* (student answer). In my opinion this change meant that on one hand they became more realistic concerning their professional goals on the other hand they got engaged a bit more, started to 'plan with' and think about the professions they are studying now.

- After the first year of the theoretical training the respondents' opinion was all in all more positive about the theoretical part than after the beginning of the training. While at the beginning one of them was very dissatisfied with the scope of theory lessons now all of them found it very satisfactory.
- At the beginning two of the students thought that they cannot apply the knowledge gained in theory classes in practice, by the end of the year most of them strongly agreed with the well-applicability of theory classes in practice.
- **The lack of connection between theory and practice was the most criticized part of the training program by students, instructors and lecturers equally.**
- A great improvement compared to the beginning of the course was that while at the beginning 37,5% of the students found themselves rather or strongly unprepared for the practice after the theoretical classes, at the end of the year all those students who responded at least 'rather agreed' that they are prepared for practice after theory. One of them even gave a written remark: *'on the theory lesson the teacher explains it very well and it got stuck in my mind'.*
- Important information is that by the end of the year **all respondents found the theoretical training rather too long.** Although all respondents agreed that the 1 year of the training is satisfactory. Most of them were satisfied with the structure of the training about ¼ at school and ¾ in the company, although one of the respondents found it rather dissatisfying. It is very promising that after the one year long training **all respondents felt well prepared to start working on the job market.** They were rather differing opinions if they recommended the training for their friends or not. One of them even explained that *'I would not recommend it to my friend only because he is not enough prepared and responsible for this training'.*

- **Almost all students reported a greater need for more assistance in practice.**
- By the end **the training met the expectations of all students** and most of them were at least satisfied with the training in general.
- Concerning productivity, at the end of the year there was a wider consensus among the students who responded that they are doing productive work for the company than at the beginning of the practical training.
- Concerning students' opinion about working opportunities, while at the beginning of the practical training 75% of them hoped that they can work for the company after the training, **at the end of the training all respondents hoped that they would be employed by the company.**
- The opinion about pedagogically well-preparedness of the **instructors** did not change. The **majority of the students perceived that they are well-prepared**. It is the same about getting an insight into all areas of activities in the company – most students strongly agreed with that at the beginning of the practical training and they had the same opinion by the end.

Survey with the enterprises

The assessment of the Hamburg Model training at the end of the training period, the instructors' opinion was very much in line with what they have reported at the beginning of the practical training in all questions. Therefore in this part only the answers will be picked out and represented which differ to the ones at the beginning.

- **Enterprises were not fully satisfied with the connection between theory and practice**, which need analyse of the work between the school and enterprises and an improvement implementing the Hamburg Model next time.
- Almost all instructors are agreed that **the Hamburg Model-based vocational education is a realistic scenario for Hungary in the future.**
- Contrary to some instructors' opinion at the beginning about the ratio of the theory and practice, by the end of the training year both instructors strongly agreed that the ratio of practice and theory is appropriate.

- The instructors rather agreed or strongly agreed that students are well-suited for the training.
- Both instructors found their pedagogical education level appropriate for the task of instructing and supervising the students.
- The instructors strongly agreed that the original aims of the training were clear.
- Instructors were more convinced (in comparison at the beginning of the training) that their company wants to employ a participant/participants after completing the training (they rather agreed at that time and they absolutely agreed at the end of the training).
- **There was a wide consensus that the students contribute productively to the company** already during the training.
- They would have recommended other companies to participate in this professional training and were **all in all very pleased with the training so far, which met their expectations.**

Survey with the lecturers

- The majority, four lecturers assessed the ratio of theory and practice appropriate at the end of the training period. One lecturer had strong concerns against it.
- Just like at the beginning of the training, there was a full consensus among the theoretical lecturers that **the exchange with the enterprises is good and the practically learned skills, experiences and knowledge can be well applied in the theoretical training**.
- The lecturers were still **critical concerning the suitability** of the students for the training: at the end of the training still three teachers out of five thought that the participants are not well-suited for this training and only two of them agreed about the students' suitability.
- The lecturers' opinion differed about the course premises, facilities and equipment: the majority of them see those rather unsuitable for the needs of the training. It may be caused due to the fact that there lacks of needed equipment mentioned before, and two teachers assess it as appropriate.

- Surprisingly in comparison to the responses of the enterprises the teachers rather have doubts about the productivity of the students work for the company while learning: while at the beginning all teachers considered the students work productive for the company at the end of the training two teachers has doubts about that.
- All of the teachers would recommend other schools to implement the Hamburg Model-based vocational training.
- **Finally the vast majority of the lecturers found the model as an adequate answer to the challenges of the Hungarian vocational educational system.**
- The most of the lecturers believed that the implementation of the Hamburg Model into the Hungarian vocational training system is a realistic goal.

7. Recommendations for implementation of the Hamburg Model[30]

The following main points need to be taken into account implementing the Hamburg Model:

- The Hamburg Model should offer or open continuation of vocational training, since the Hamburg Model is quickly misunderstood as one-year, completed vocational training. But this is not the case. It is a model for the integration of young people, who have not received professional training course after completion of general education, into three to three and a half years of vocational training. The one-year training with specific consulting,

---

[30] The recommendations result from the following reports: J. E. Radder / M. Rominger, (HI 23, HI 21-14), Draft – State as of 20 September 2012, 3:00 pm, Report of the Working Group 'Vocational Qualification', September 2012, pp. 13 – 17; Implementation report for Lithuania by Renata Cerneckiene; Implementation report for Hungary by Laszlo Kajos and Istvan Mosoczi.

support and integration measures in the context of the Hamburg Model can represent the first year of training, but can also be an additional training peri-period which is followed by the three to three and a half years of vocational training. After completing the one-year training phase of the Hamburg Mod-Model at least 75-80% of the participants can be integrated into a regular vocational training. For the then not yet integrated youth more funding and special measures are to be used, for example, a vocational training in inter-company training workshops. The aim is that no one will be outsourced and 100% young people receive vocational training.

- The Hamburg Model is a "guided training" where the trainees are supported and supervised by trainers at school (or other specialists, e.g. social workers, etc.) during the whole training; it is the responsibility of the school; it includes regular visits of participants at extra school training centers, for example, and support especially in problem situations at the enterprise, consultations on the choice of the suitable profession.

- The training need to be provided in professions for which there is demand in specialists at the labour market, the target group fulfils the admission prerequisites of the dual vocational training and the needs of the cooperative training model can be satisfied, namely the training places in enterprises are available.

- The training should be provided in recognised professions within the meaning of the individual country's law.

- Depending on the country conditions, it is favourable (even needed, see the country reports of implementation from Lithuania and Hungary), when training is (co-)financed by public funding.

- The Hamburg Model shall ease the entry into vocational education and training. It is designed for so called "market disadvantaged" young people, who possibly have difficulties in the theoretical lessons but otherwise have good practical skills, who do not find a training opportunity and thus stay in long queues. This group of youth is the priority group for which the training should be offered. However, the detailed preconditions of the target group should be set according to the country conditions and needs. For all together the primary requirement is that the target group has reached training maturity. The absent training maturity at the moment of application for Hamburg Model can be achieved at a later moment – during the professional qualification.

- There need to be signed an educational contract which determines the goals of the training in the Hamburg Model and the rights and obligations of the school and also participants and cooperation contract with the enterprises.

- The weekly working and educational time at school, at the enterprise and at the corporate training facilities is guided by corresponding labour agreements; as a rule it includes 38 – 40 hours; the practical training can also take place during school holidays.

- The practical and school based part should correspond to the dual education principles – 25 % theory at school, 75 % practice at enterprise, at corporate training centers and/or at school workshops); however, the proportional division can vary according to the profession; however, the practice part must predominate.

- According to the Hamburg Model there must be at least 2 not profession related subjects that intend to develop competencies.

- The training must be carried out in close cooperation with enterprises, chambers and professional associations to coordinate the responsibilities and exchange between these participating parties during the training.

- Application procedure and qualifying conditions (date for application, the needed documents, etc.) are determined according to the country specific conditions. Here the cooperation between e. g. the school and employment agency is necessary.

- If the school do not have permanent enterprises with whom it cooperates to train the trainees, the acquisition of the enterprises for the training need to be started in due time.

- It is possible to introduce half a year probation period.

- The performance results of participants are evaluated with marks. The practical training is evaluated by the corresponding enterprise or the cooperate training center. The performance results of participants with marks are indicated in certificates which the training participants receive in case of successful participation.

- Offering and implementing the Hamburg Model it is important to inform and consult the target groups and the involved parties of the Hamburg Model. For these purposes in framework of the project a flyer as one of the information instruments was developed and distributed.

Take your chance!

Hanse-Parlament is an association of more than 50 chambers of crafts, industry and commerce and other institutions supporting Small- and Medium Sized Enterprises (SMEs) in the Baltic Sea Region and has been working together since 1994.

Baltic Sea Academy is a network of 18 universities and polytechnics around the Baltic Sea.

Together they offer solutions for SMEs, especially focusing on development, implementation and transfer of educational measures like Hamburg Model.

For more information:
In Germany
Hanse-Parlament: www.hanse-parlament.eu
Baltic Sea Academy: www.balticsea-academy.eu
Hamburg Institut of Vocational Education (HIBB): www.hibb.hamburg.de
In Latvia
Chamber of Crafts: www.lak.lv
In Lithuania
Vilnius Builder Trainings Center: www.vsrc.lt
In Norway
Nordic Forum of Crafts: www.nhforum.org
In Poland
Hanseatic Academy of Management in Slupsk: www.whsz.slupsk.pl
In Hungary
Kontiki Vocational Training AG: www.kontikizrt.hu

Entry into the dual vocational training -
New chance for young people and enterprises

What is the dual vocational training?

The dual system of vocational training consists of two parts: a theoretical part in a vocational training facility (1/3) and a **practical part (2/3)** in an enterprise. Thus, young people learn the practical work from the beginning and enterprises get young professionals with a tailor-made qualification they seek.

What is the Hamburg Training Model?

Hamburg Institute of Vocational Education in Hamburg, Germany developed the Hamburger Training Model, where it has been successfully implemented for five years.

It is a proven method to integrate young people into the professional education, who would otherwise not get this chance. While or after one year of learning the students can continue with the regular dual professional education.

What does the professional education training contain and on what terms can it be conducted?

The training begins with classes at the respective vocational school for a few weeks. Then, the participating students pass different company and school based learning phases. The young people receive intensive advising, learn about enterprises and different professions, choose a professional training and get the corresponding training place.

The „entry" by the Hamburg Training Model in vocational training is provided up to one year, after that the young people continue the regular vocational training in the chosen profession.

This first year can be credited to the entire training period.

The teaching and learning contents match those of the first year of the training in the dual system of vocational training.

What are the objectives of the project?

Within the project "Perspective Future: One Year Professional Qualification" the Hamburg Model will be transferred to other countries, adapted to the needs of the individual countries to be implemented there.

How can young people take part in the professional training?

Young people need a certificate of general education

Why should young people and businesses join in?

- Enterprises get to know the youngsters over longer time and
- Learning the profession under real conditions in a company
- Improvement of chances on the labour market

Why should enterprises join?

- **Enterprises get to know the youngsters over longer time and**
- At the same time **familiarise** the young people with the work in the own company
- They find **excellent skilled professionals with precisely-fitting qualification**

HANSE-PARLAMENT
Network for Small and Medium Enterprises

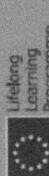

Lifelong
Learning
Programme

8. Outlook

8.1. Feasibility studies for three Sub regions of the Province of Pomerania by Hanseatic Academy of Management in Slupsk[31]

In the project the implementation of the Hamburg Model was planned in the countries: Poland, Lithuania or Hungary. After extensive research and negotiations it turned out that an implementation in Poland due to legal reasons is not possible. This is why the Hamburg Model was realized in Lithuania and Hungary. However, for Poland the possibilities of the implementation of the Hamburg Model and the introduction of the dual vocational training were examined as well as which regulatory changes need to be made and in which steps the realization can be done.

The results of this feasibility study are shown in the following chapter.

8.1.1. Introduction

In Poland the amount of the expenditure on research - developmental activity in the relation to the GDP for years continues on the level similar to the 0,5% (in years 2005 - 2006 it was 0,6 - 0,7 %). In UE - 27 he amounts to average expenses on R+D about 2,1%. For many years over the 40% of the expenditure they are giving research centres being in a Mazowian province (in 2006 in counting per capita PLN 450), and

---

[31] Michał Igielski, PhD, Monika Zajkowska, PhD, *Feasibility studies - three Subregions of the Province of Pomerania* (desk research), unpublished paper; Slupsk, 2014.

on Pomerania this amount amounts about PLN 200. One should also notice, that regions of Europe Baltic (on the level NUTS 3) in the very uneven grade funds are discounting from the European Union for the innovative activity. Amongst 15 regions the EU which are giving no less than a 3,5% to the GDP to the research and development, 6 regions are located in Germany, 4 in Sweden and 3 in Finland. Remaining are spending much below the desirable level (including the Pomeranian province). And one should mark, that from structural funds of the over 86 bn euro (25% of funds from ERDF) intended is for innovative projects both in the area of the technology as well as the development of enterprises and innovative organizations. In Poland the participation of innovative enterprises in the sector of industrial enterprises at the end of the 20th century exceeded little over the 17%, while at that time the average for 15 EU countries developed on the level exceeding the 50%. At the beginning of the 21st century (in 2002 - 2004 years) the share of innovative enterprises amongst Polish industrial enterprises rose to the level of the 26,6%, and in 27 states reduced up to the 41 - 5% - results from examinations of the Central Statistical Office (polish: GUS) and the Eurostat[32].

In terms of the innovative activity Polish enterprises are outdistancing only companies from Malta, Romania, Hungary, Bulgaria and Latvia. Such a situation results not only from the capital weakness Polish enterprises. To important reasons an unreadiness of staffs and graduates of our vocational schools ranks among innovative actions. It is result of also very weak connections of enterprises with the educational environment. The financing structure of research - developmental action in Poland is opposite than in UE - 27. He isn't fulfilling even assumptions made in

---

[32] On the basis of data the GUS and the Eurostat - downloaded from sides www.epp.eurostat.ec.europa.eu/portal and www.stat.gov.pl

the Lisbon Strategy, according to which two thirds of expenditure on R+D should come from the private sector.

Pomerania is reflecting such a situation, where from analysis of Development Strategy 2020 and the Development Strategy of the Country and SWOT analyses included in them it results that they are barriers of the economic development of the region: low economic competitiveness of companies, lack of the consistent system of the promotion of entrepreneurship, low level of investment, poor innovative culture, lack of connecting the education with needs of the labour market. He is happening this way, because the Pomeranian province is characterized relating to remaining provinces by a minute number of special acting institutions for supporting the sector SMEs in the field of preparing new releases and examinations. Nothing so strange also granting the advanced of the support for the vocational education rarely meets in order to build the competitive edge based on innovations.

One should consider the being of the vocational education above all in the context of the labour market - it is such a part of the entire educational system, for which he is a task direct preparing for pursuing a definite profession. Therefore it is worthwhile thinking, whether it is gifted in our country for educating graduates adapted to conditioning of the contemporary economic system, being able to find their place on the labour market and gaining recognizing employers rapidly.

On account of:
- dynamic changes in the demand for the work which require the significant big flexibility along with the occupational mobility;
- substantial reduction of the significance of traditional economic branches to the benefit of the ones new and innovative, where often (completely exaggeratedly) a higher education is expected; vocational education, should in the more active and dynamic way participate in processes occurring in the sphere economically - social.

Very vocational education has in the Pomeranian province, in particular outside areas of major cities long-standing tradition well important very often has at his disposal an enormous potential which must be used to the purpose of the efficiency improvement of the regional labour market, what will certainly be transferred into the growth in the economy. Unfortunately long-term negligence connected with popularizing the secondary school education, they caused, that the reactivation of this process required immediate and system corrective actions in order to rise the vocational training from the crisis it was in which.

In this situation he can turn out to be one of medicines, very much valued in other European countries and more and more often being a subject of nationwide discussion, model of dual educating the profession, understood as[33]: *combining the knowledge acquisition at school and the practical learning of the specific profession in the enterprise.*

Unfortunately in spite of such great interest in this system the knowledge to his subject along with the possible implementation plan and determining barriers and potential advantages for entities employed in it is still too small and very much dispersed. The lack is also in this discussion, differently comprehend the shared voice system bodies running schools, their employees (not to say pupils), and entrepreneurs, labour market institutions, not to say representatives of individual political groups.

8.1.2. Characteristics of sub regions from pose of the metropolis Tricity in the Pomeranian province

According to assumptions of the Strategy of 2020, four sub regions are included in a Pomeranian province: Metropolitarny, Słupski, Południowy, Nadwiślański. For the

---

[33] J. Wiktorowicz, *Talent in practice - vocational training*, Final report, Łódź 2013.

purposes of this study, to begin with, a presented descriptive character sketch of three sub regions, suiting the Tricity metropolis outside area will stay.

8.1.2.1. Słupski Sub region[34]

The Słupski Sub region is spreading through the area of three districts - Słupsk, Lębork and Bytów and city of Słupsk. The total aggregate area of the Słupsk sub region is 5245 km^2 , and 25 communes and the city of Słupsk are entering his composition. The area of the Słupski Sub region is being inhabited is through close 335 000 of persons. The average unemployment rate in the Słupski Sub region is taking out over 19 %. The performed work for the generality of people is the meat and potatoes in the life, deciding on the level of the affluence, and consequently, place and residential conditions or generally comprehended satisfaction. In this sub region it is possible to regard as important factors affecting the labour market:

- minute number of situations vacant falling on the 100 unemployed;
- low indicator of the employment in market services;
- high unemployment rate;
- relatively low pays in comparing e.g. to Tricity.

Table No. 1: List of institutions carrying the vocational training out in the school system in the Słupski Sub region.

---

[34] On the base: Results of the work of the Słupsk Sub region Working Team - update of the Development Strategy of the Province of Pomerania 2014-2020, Słupsk 2014.

Source: own study on the base: of List of nursery schools, schools and an educational institutions in the Pomeranian province, Education Office of the in Gdańsk, according to the state as on the 30.09.2013 day.

	fundamental vocational schools	technical secondary schools	vocational colleges
Słupsk district	1	2	3
Lębork district	4	5	7
Bytów district	4	5	6
City of Słupsk	11	14	24
Sum	**20**	**26**	**40**

8.1.2.2. Południowy Sub region[35]

The Południowy Sub region is spreading through the area of three districts - Chojnice, Człuchów and Kościerzyna. The total aggregate area of the south sub region is 4105 km², and 19 communes and city of Chojnice are entering his composition, Człuchów and Kościerzyna. The area of the Południowy Sub region is being inhabited is through close 225 000 of persons. The average unemployment rate in the sub region is taking out over 15 %. As the most crucial issue for the entire region a very low level of the entrepreneurship which many factors affect, is determined among others communications availability which is a great impediment

---

[35] On the base: - Results of the work of the Południowy Sub region Working Team - update of the Development Strategy of the Province of Pomerania 2014-2020, Człuchów 2014.

for the productive activity. Also high labour costs are affecting the entrepreneurship level. Local entrepreneurs aren't able efficiently to act based on existing institutions of the business environment which largely are functional outside the area of this sub region.

Table No. 2: List of institutions carrying the vocational training out in the school system in the Południowy Sub region.

	fundamental vocational schools	technical secondary schools	vocational colleges
Chojnice district	6	7	8
Człuchów district	3	9	2
Kościerzyna district	5	4	4
Sum	**14**	**20**	**14**

Source: own study on the base: of List of nursery schools, schools and an educational institutions in the Pomeranian province, Education Office of the in Gdańsk, according to the state as on the 30.09.2013 day.

8.1.2.3. Nadwiślański Sub region[36]

The Nadwiślański Sub region is spreading through the area of five districts - Malbork, Kwidzyn, Tczew, Sztum, and Starogard Gdański. The total aggregate area of the Nadwiślański Sub region is 4102 km², and 29 communes and cities Malbork, Kwidzyn, Tczew, Sztum, Starogard Gdański are access into his composition. The area of the Nadwiślański Sub region is being inhabited through close 435 000 of persons. The average unemployment rate in the Nadwiślański Sub region is taking out close the 20%. As the biggest developmental barriers for this region which the most are blocking his development, social crash barriers are being replaced in the form of low and much diversified profits of local households which result on the fact of the persistence of the high rate of the structural unemployment.

Table No. 3: List of institutions carrying the vocational training out in the school system in the Nadwiślański Sub region.

	fundamental vocational schools	technical secondary schools	vocational colleges
Malbork district	3	3	2
Kwidzyn district	6	4	10
Tczew district	8	5	8
Sztum district	3	3	4
Starogard Gdański district	5	9	15

---

[36] On the base: Results of the work of the Nadwiślański Sub region Working Team - update of the Development Strategy of the Province of Pomerania 2014-2020, Starogard Gdański 2014.

| Sum | 25 | 24 | 39 |

Source: own study on the base: of List of nursery schools, schools and an educational institutions in the Pomeranian province, Education Office of the in Gdańsk, according to the state as on the 30.09.2013 day.

8.1.3. System of the vocational education - the current state and crucial problems

8.1.3.1. Vocational education in Poland

From 1989, along with beginning political transformations and the structural readjustment in Poland in the economy, we are observing into the systematic debasement of the system of the vocational training. His social and system marginalization is manifesting itself above all in the mass liquidation of vocational schools, factory schools and the base of the practical training (of school workshops). These changes in part were an effect widely snitch and of dynamic structural and property transformations from one side, whereas on the other with gradual spreading among the masses educating on the higher education. Today, after 25 years of market transformations (in it also concerning an educational system), the vocational education is in the relatively bad general position. The system of the vocational training demonstrates certain inertia towards changes on the labour market. These ones are largely a consequence of radical changes in the size and the structure of the demand for the work reported by entrepreneurs. The base of the vocational education is most often outdated if to take the state of capital assets into consideration (buildings, technical base and the like), directions and contents of the education aren't adapted for current needs and requirements of the market, but pupils of many vocational schools leaving them as graduates without undergoing traineeships. Additionally how, of the Central Statistical Office results from data analyses concerning the vocational training in the Pomeranian province, scarcely the 33%[37] of pupils of vocational schools indeed is finishing them[38].

Vocational training in the school system is being carried out at fundamental vocational schools, technical secondary schools (in it supplementing) and at vocational colleges. Preparing for pursuing a definite profession is an aim of the education of this type[39].

Leaving the school and passing an examination enable to obtain the certificate confirming professional qualifications. With legal document, based on which the school curriculum and standards of requirements underlying conducting the examination confirming professional qualifications are arising, there is a programme base. The ministry of the Education is implementing also modular school curricula as well as with the approval of employer organizations or economic self-governments is carrying action out in the practical apprenticeship. Vocational schools can educate the Minister of National Education in 208 disappointments defined in the Regulation from 16 July 2008. The competition is being entered into classification to the conclusion appropriate (determined in the regulation) of minister. The level of taking control of the message and abilities from the scope of the given profession is being assessed through the examination confirming professional qualifications. This examination is conducted once within one year school in the period from the June up to the August. He consists of two stages: of the written part and the practical part. Principles of operation of the earlier economic system supported the development of the educational system, in which the education underwent oneself in narrow

---

[37] On the basis of data GUS for 2013 - downloaded from the side www.stat.gov.pl
[38] E. Lechman, *Dual system of the vocational training in Poland - chances and barriers of the implementation* (expert opinion), Gdańsk 2012
[39] On the base given from the side www.koweziu.edu.pl/faq_print.php

specializations, adapted to the work in the specific profession. Schools closely were connected with state - owned enterprises, enabling thorough determining the demand for employees in the process comparatively about given qualifications. The vocational education performed the particularly important role in frames functioning in those times, set mainly to the industrial production, of economic policy. In Poland a high percentage of persons beginning the professional learning, of narrow scope of the specialization marked beginnings of a systemic transformation and the degree very much limited of teaching theoretical bases, associated with a given field of knowledge. Educated graduates according to the above model weren't prepared for changes of occupation associated with dynamic changes in the structure and the production technology. Of transforming in the business world and social caused that a crisis had afflicted the vocational education. Very much a difficult situation economic, associated with the significant drop in production and a rise in unemployment was catalyst for negative trends appearing in this period. A drastic decrease in national expenses on the vocational education took place; the considerable part of enterprises wasn't in funds for the staff training and for employing the new staff. Simultaneously with the appearance of above phenomena a demand for employees fell about the vocational secondary education. In the Polish economy a service industry gained the more and more great significance, while the industry sector lost its dominant position. Prospects of the great unemployment and low pays for graduates of vocational schools, as well as negative social perception of the vocational education interests in this form of education caused the significant decrease[40].

---

[40] Ł. Pyfel, R. Jaros, P. Krajewski, M. Wochna, *Recommendations concerning needs in the vocational education*, INSE, Warszawa 2010.

8.1.3.2. Problems of the vocational education in the Pomeranian province

Vocational education in order to educate on appropriately the highest level, using new technologies and adapting to dynamic changes on the labour market, requires incurring the considerable financial outlays. The technical equipment of schools should still be updated in order to keep up behind incessant changes in the technology. Problems in financing vocational schools concern also a teaching staff. Low pays in it are letting down, that best qualified persons are going to better of paid employment in the private sector. The vocational education by the current funding level isn't able to meet requirements of specialist educating of persons prepared for taking up work directly on completion the learning. In this respect cooperation with enterprises is a rational solution in training, at exploiting the infrastructure held by them, devices and the staff, instead of investing considerable financial means in institutions conditions trying to imitate or to simulate ruling in the real workplace. Essential however in functioning of the vocational education a mechanism which would provide with stimuli for recognizing the demand of the labour market is an aspect (instead of costs) as the priority of qualifications in decisions to conduct the learning determined[41].

To sum up, in the last report from examinations concerning functioning of the system of the vocational training in the province Pomeranian, commissioned by the Ministry of National Education, clearly his main problems to which they belong were shown[42]:

---

[41] Ibidem.

[42] *Examining functioning of the system of the vocational training in Poland.* Final report, Ministry of National Education, National Centre of supporting the vocational education and Constant, Warszawa 2012.

a) Few vocational schools and the Centre of the Practical Education (CPE, polish: CKP) offer the program which would be adapted for the actual demand reported on the side of employers to their pupils.
b) Too general and theoretical program of educating at school which in the bottom stair is preparing the graduate of a vocational school for taking up work.
c) The minute number of directors of vocational schools is declaring the responsiveness with outside institutions dealing with issues of the labour market.
d) Poorly spread - system of the careers guidance. In individuals of the vocational training an effective system of the consulting is missing educational - professional, which current diagnosing the level of education of pupils and their professional predispositions would be possible thanks to.
e) The structure of the demand for the work is maladjusted to the supply of the work. The largest percentage of institutions of the vocational training offers the education at present on directions: catering and of food production, mechanical, electric, electronic, teleinformatic. However the keen demand for the work on the part of employers exists for educating on directions: economic, financially - office, building, road and of construction installations, transport, of inventory management.
f) Employers have a lot of trouble finding employees with suitable qualifications.
g) The forming of the educational offer of vocational schools in the biggest measuring cup is being determined with the back had by a given institution and the equipment required for the practical accomplishment and the available staff.

8.1.3.3. Meaning of the dual system of the vocational training

From experience of such economies like Germany, Switzerland, or Austria, it is possible to come to the conclusion, that imposed solutions formal and legal, regulating the education system from one side, whereas on the other, throwing frameworks for cooperation between the sphere of entrepreneurs and the educational sphere, can in the significant way contribute to the smooth functioning of the labour market. He is an example of such a system termination dual (alternating) system of the vocational training. This system is regarded as the system answer allowing for improving efficiency of functioning of the labour market, above all from a point of view of employers. He is an idea of the dual system of the vocational training parallel - two way - educating at a vocational school, where the pupil is acquiring the theoretical knowledge above all, and in the chosen workplace, where is undergoing the practical apprenticeship. An adaptation of plots of the teaching is a fundamental advantage of this solution (structure of the general theoretical and practical plan of the education) to actual needs of entrepreneurs (that is of reported demand for the work) what are possible thanks to the flow of information between entrepreneurs and vocational schools. Taking the cooperation between these two groups of market subjects causes, that schools are educating in the competition to which he exists real of demand on the local labour market. In the process it prevents coming into existence of the structural unemployment in the economy[43].

To sum up, in all systems of the dual education he is standing out with the close cooperation of schools and employers. In the assumed typology it is possible to indicate in the European Union[44]:

- vocational training full time teachings (France, Italy, Belgium) - a state which is financing them from public means is responsible for the education;
- vocational training and alternating (Great Britain) - the pupil is acquiring the professional knowledge at school or on course, next is getting practical skills in enterprises;

---

[43] E. Lechman, *Dual system of the vocational training in Poland - chances and barriers of the implementation* (expert opinion), Gdańsk 2012.

[44] On the base E. Goźlińska, *Diploma for the European Examination confirming professional qualifications after the technical vocational school and the post-secondary non-tertiary education,* Guide for pupils, a Central examination board, Warszawa 2009, downloaded from the side www.zst.cieszyn.pl/mechatplc_mechatr/dyplom_dla_europejczyka.pdf.

- vocational training with full hours of teaching at school in combination with teaching in the enterprise (Luxembourg, Ireland, Netherlands) - the part of classes is adapted to needs of the enterprise;
- vocational training based on educating in the enterprise (Denmark, Germany, Austria) - the pupil within the week is studying for 1-2 days at a vocational school, and then for 3-4 days in the so-called enterprise dualism.

From a microeconomic point of view, benefits from implementing the dual educa-education system are mutual, both for entrepreneurs and for very pupils[45]:
1. From the perspective of the enterprise:
- the entrepreneur is educating the pupil according to personal needs, requirements and standards. Many entrepreneurs are holding a view that it is hard to find on the market of the person, fully fulfilling requirements put by them - qualifications, practical experience, personality features.
- the employer has an option of pupil enrolled for the practice what is minimizing mistakes (incorrect decisions) committed often at the standard recruitment;
- the fact that companies enrolling pupils to traineeships are gaining the right to use the logo with the inscription is an important component of taking part in the dual system by the entrepreneur: *this enterprise is educating* what is treated as the advertising form (marketing action). Entrepreneurs are gaining the reputation on the labour market what is having a positive effect for noticing their company on the market (corporate social responsibility).
- entrepreneurs perceive the participation in the vocational training as long - term investments into own employees;
- recruiting the relatively cheap employee;
- the system enables to provide professions for the continuity - concerns to above all of craft sector, where traditions are playing the particular role.

---

[45] E. Lechman, *Dual system of the vocational training in Poland - chances and barriers of the implementation* (expert opinion), Gdańsk 2012.

2. From the perspective of pupils:
- the pupil is getting experiencing directly at the potential future employer;
- for pupils of vocational schools a fluid passage from the period of the learning to the active working life enables the system;
- the offer of schools strongly is fitted to needs and requirements of the labour market (it is the fundamental assumption of functioning of the dual system) what he/she is marking, that the majority of pupils on the level of vocational schools won't be taking the research up in professions which are a demand missing on the part of employers or he is very low;
- undergoing the work practice in the enterprise which is complying with the requirements of the contemporary market;
- the pupil has a possibility of the active participation in the manufacturing cycle of the enterprise what constitutes the additional value given from a point of view of the undergone educational process;
- the system enables the forming of attitudes and competence which are being thought highly by their future employers. To so it is possible among others to rank: enterprising conducts, the respect and the respect for the performed work, shaped loyalty to the workplace, responsibility for entrusted tasks, desire for the further education and raising qualifications.
3. From the perspective of the total economy:
- education effective system of the vocational training which is preparing young people for pursuing a specific profession;
- existence of the system solution which employing graduates of vocational schools is facilitating;
- liberalizing the labour market;
- undertaking the interaction between entrepreneurs and educational institutions in relation to defining directions and forms of the vocational training according to the current demand on the labour market.

To sum up a dual education is a model of the teaching, in which the cooperation of vocational schools with entrepreneurs is playing the key role. It is system, which similarly like other has determined defects, as well as virtues. Accustoming him in one piece or only him of chosen elements is dependent from many factors, in it among others of social factors and economic. In Poland the model of the education wearing hallmarks of the dual system successfully functioned at factory schools. At present he is appearing as part of the craft competition. Very much effectively he operates in Western European countries (in it among others in Germany, Switzerland, and Austria). Best practices from our neighbours successfully can constitute the inspiration for action taken in our area. In the dual system the pupil is acquiring the knowledge at school, next is purchasing abilities in the workplace. This model assumes that young people within the week are spending a few days in the educational establishment and a few days at the employer. Also a heavy responsibility of pupils is characteristic of him for the process of getting competence - because it is they are finding the employer for themselves and are signing the agreement with him for practice. Simultaneously they receive the remuneration for the provided work, as well as for them appropriate benefits are being paid. The graduate educated in this way has qualifications adapted for demands for the labour market, on completion a professional experience already has schools and in this way is becoming more competitive on the market. According to assumptions of the dual education the role of employers isn't only confining itself to make places available for practice. Because entrepreneurs briskly are employed into other activity aimed at improving efficiency of the vocational training, in it among others by creating school curricula, the participation in the examination process of pupils or investing financial means. In this way employers are educating their future employees in line with their expectations, equipping them with essential competence in of them, be related, workplaces. Next educating vocational schools in the dual system are becoming more attractive on the market of the education[46].

Implementing the dual education in the Pomeranian province for deciding large scale than so far requires not isolated action but creating the process thought over

---

[46] Ibidem.

which to begin with would verify real opportunities of functioning of this system and would enable fluent basics and functioning. They must be it is action however taken not only on the regional but also nationwide level:

- on the regional level:, first, establishing the body dealing with points of order and the organization and promoting is shown of cooperation of vocational schools with entrepreneurs;
- on the nationwide level: one should above all establish legal norms of his functioning and principles of financing;
- on the local level: a need of disseminating and creating the positive image of the dual education exists.

8.1.3.4. German model of the dual vocational training

In the German education system dual a few kinds of schools participate. To put it simply they are it appropriately:

- primary school: for pupils aged 6-10;
- secondary school of the first degree - equivalent of the Polish junior secondary school: for pupils in the century 10-15 / 16 years;
- educating vocational schools in the dual system: half of dimension of the time of the learning (51%), in the full dimension of the time (12%) and secondary schools of the second degree equivalent of the Polish secondary school (37%) - for pupils aged 15-19.

Above the person 19 of year of age of the May to choose from carrying the learning on as part of the higher education system (university) or the market penetration of the work and possible using the system of the continuing vocational training. Very much undergone traineeship of enterprises is a crucial element of the dual education system. Apart from different types of schools, the German system of the post-secondary vocational education is based on a cooperation of many partners. Apart from different types of schools, the German system of the post - secondary vocational education is based on a cooperation of many partners. The all sorts entities involved in this process are accepting different functions and areas of responsibility resulting from them to themselves. Moreover both a procedure of seeking practice by trainee graduates of the profession, and then undergoing very practice are playing the particular role[47].

German model of the vocational education, so - called dual system (double check system) connecting the theoretical learning with the practical vocational training which constitutes a preliminary vocational training course is establishing. Persons getting the vocational secondary education by way of the dual education most often undergo the three-year-old apprenticeship at school and in the workplace according to the chosen profession or at specialist vocational schools being subject to an exclusive control of the State. Into the education system dual in Germany are involved both partners from the federal level, as well as from the Land level. That is essentially are if: you are social partners (representatives of employers and employees) and industrial and sales chambers or craft chambers. On the federal level they are the state agencies involved in the system of the dual vocational training above all Ministry of Research and of Education and the Labor Department and Economies. On the federal level establishing the general rules concerning the organization of the educational process is a responsibility of the state post-secondary. These principles assumed the form of the Act on a vocational training course (Berufsbildungsgesetz). According to records of this act, regulations of the learning set by all representatives of groups involved in the process are being put into practice by the competent minister on the rung of the federation - most often of minister for the economy. A job classification being in force is an essential attachment of the act which in 2001 counted 360 professions. The dual system doesn't include the civil service, partly also

---

[47] A. Kwiatkiewicz, *Vocational education in the German dual system,* E-mentor No. 1 (13) / 2006, downloaded from the side www.e-mentor.edu.pl/artykul/index/numer/13/id/245

of practiced professions in the department of the health. It is worthwhile noticing, that when the act on a vocational training course came into effect over 30 years ago, the service sector had a lower significance than in times of those present far and therefore the professions typical of the service sector in it weren't also considered. According to the discussed act as part of the dual system leaving a ten-year-old secondary modern school is a condition of the learning. Being characteristic of federal regulations in the field of the lifelong education one should mention The Vocational Training Act which educating young person's leaving the system of the compulsory learning is regulating. This document determines that the vocational training is combining the education preliminary, retraining the lifelong education and programs. According to the German constitution regulations arising from this act don't influence functioning of vocational schools which are left in the management of individual Lands[48].

The German system obliges all enterprises to form a union at the chamber industrial and provident, but doesn't oblige them to enroll pupils for practice. In spite of the lack of such a legal requirement, the majority of companies is enrolling pupils for practice regarding it as a natural course of events. In this place it is worthwhile emphasizing cultural conditioning of the system dual, having its roots in the 19th century and coming from the craft. The long - standing tradition caused that they had felt names and still, in most cases, are feeling obliged to accept trainee graduates of the profession for practice, even in the light of the lack of official regulations of this issue which would impose such a duty upon them. It is possible so to put the thesis forward about voluntary, conditioned with tradition, for joining in of enterprises into the process of the vocational education. He is happening this way, because the system of practice allows for the education relatively with modest cost of the specific number of young people acquainted with practical aspects of the work, rather than only with

---

[48] Ibidem.

her theoretical part. It is worthwhile adding that through the entire duration of the practice the enterprise is using the work provided by the cheaper employee. Additional advantages of this system are a real influence of enterprises on the offer and a manner of the organization of the system of the vocational education, and in the end to competence of graduates. Differently a situation is in the case young, of unskilled workers. Apart from the voluntary support on the part of employers, the dual system additionally is enhanced with federal regulations which are imposing an obligation to finance or to support the organization of trainings for representatives of this group on employers. Enterprises can sign agreements as part of their sectors or also industries. Such sector agreements - strengthened with federal and domestic regulations - they cause, that thanks to the fairly incurred expenditure on trainings a threat of buying trained employees is reducing, and very training is perceived as the value added about the both individual and collective nature[49].

8.1.3.5. Situation of graduates of schools carrying the vocational training out in the school system on the Pomeranian labour market

It became a fact that the higher education stopped being only and exclusively a privilege and a pass for finding a well - paid job. At present for the higher education he is having access almost everyone. The universal aspiration to receiving a diploma is finding its reflection in statistics. While on the beginning of the decade 259 thousand graduates left Polish colleges, it is in 2010 this number grew to almost 475 thousand that is almost twice. It is worthwhile noticing that in 2010 it left walls of the college over 312 thousand of women. Representatives of the fair sex decided as many as two thirds of all graduates what undoubtedly is also being transferred on proportion

---

[49] Ibidem.

amongst unemployed graduates. In terms of the number of graduates amongst Mazovian provinces is an indisputable leader. In 2010 the diploma of one of Mazovian colleges found its way to over 80 thousand persons. Next the Pomeranian province is placed on the spot 8 thousand from nearly 24 thousand of graduates[50], from which it over 1/3 cannot find no job.

Unfortunately we are also in the middle of the rate as regards people's right after vocational schools which cannot find a job. Although graduates for you are demonstrating the high activity on the labour market it is 2010 of year worked 3/4 of everyone which in the course of 12 last months left walls of a vocational school. It had problems with the placement 13% of graduates. The same percentage concerned disabled persons professionally - that is of the ones which after obtaining the certificate for different reasons didn't work or weren't interested in taking up work. However also in the Pomeranian province the positives are, because graduates of vocational schools are on the third place in the country as regards the first earnings: on average because grossed close 2500 PLN. Best graduates which found a job in the construction industry were paid. The median of their remuneration amounted to 3200 PLN. it is worthwhile will pay attention, that in second in turn of industry - light industry, earned about PLN 1200 less. The lowest pays received persons taking up work in the trade, where the median took out PLN 1800. For them greater staffing level in the company, all the higher earnings. In micro enterprises reached 2100 PLN. next in largest companies grew to 2788 PLN. Pays of persons are an exception to this rule in large firms which developed on the level 2 600 PLN[51].

---

[50] Based on information and examinations built by the Sedlak&Sedlak Company and entered into on websites: www.rynekpracy.pl, www.wynagrodzenia.pl.
[51] Ibidem.

It is worthwhile also pointing out that scarcely the 52% of pupils of vocational schools in the Pomeranian province is planning to carry the learning on. He is indicating it to the growing interest with undertaking the career as soon as possible[52]:

1. Professional plans:
   - pupils more often see themselves in the role of employees than employers - talking about one's professional plans next time are most interested in getting employing the contract of employment on principles. As far as the 80% of readings in the question about professional plans is regarding entering the contract of employment into right after the school.
   - graduates of vocational schools from their future work expect money and satisfaction from the performed job above all;
   - over half examined is admitting that he has an idea for the own business, from what as many as only 1/6 claims that the determination already has an idea for the company. However one should mark, that considerable part examined wasn't able to answer this question.
   - almost a half declaring desire for assuming own activity he isn't able still to specify, when exactly establishes an own company. Lack often shown by persons planning the business start-up of even a date moved closer and the idea for opening an own business, about the fact that they are often it is providing declarations, visions, rather than decisions serious, after all made at the moment. It can attest to the fact that the part from these persons will follow other path of the professional career.
   - the most frequent anxieties associated with conducting the own business activity concern financial matters: of costs associated with managing a company, as well as the lack of ability of the credit repayment;
   - respondents less are afraid of a bureaucracy and a lack of the equity, however much more of costs of conducting own activity.

---

[52] Based on data of the Marshall Office collected by Pentor International Poznań in 2010.

2. Assessment of the programme of classes:
- upper secondary schools than graduates aren't preparing for establishing an own company and for becoming known on the Pomeranian labour market, what's more, are more skeptical in evaluations of preparing by an educational system for managing an own company.
- over the half of pupils claims that because of that he isn't having chances of the placement in the taught profession.

8.1.3.6. Barriers and hampering of the implementing the dual system of the vocational training in the Pomeranian province

On 19 August 2011, an amended act on the educational system which is modifying conditions for the functioning of the vocational education came into effect. This act provides, that starting from school year 2012/2013, will be be able to undergo the vocational training at a three-year-old fundamental vocational school, where the entire cycle of the learning will close with obtaining the diploma confirming professional qualifications. Passing all another examinations of qualifications confirming getting necessary to pursue a given profession will be a condition of receiving a diploma. In one's assumptions reform of the vocational training, tying together being aimed the education and the work is implementing system solutions, including involving employers (by creating right mechanisms) into the educational process of pupils at a vocational school, in order to adapt qualifications for needs of the labour market[53].

It means that regulations are allowing implementing system solutions in the style of the system of the dual vocational training. However in spite of the lack of formal

---

[53] E. Lechman, *Dual system of the vocational training in Poland - chances and barriers of the implementation* (expert opinion), Gdańsk 2012.

obstacles, in our country well behind it he is going in the Pomeranian province, so far any system solutions are missing in this respect. This situation, other conditioning can mean that they exist economically - social impeding the development of this branch of the education in Poland.

It is strange, since the practical education which is held directly in a workplace, can constitute the simple solution of many current problems of the vocational education.

In fact however developing the dual education in the Pomeranian province is coming across a lot of other, more complicated barriers:
- enterprises very often aren't interested in a share in the costs of the education, in particular in periods of the significant unemployment;
- modern methods of the production, requiring the expertise, they are spelling fewer places of employment for young workers as well as require a lot of the devoted time for hands-on trainings;
- large degree of the bureaucratization.

These barriers cause that the system of practice which so far was functional in Poland, won't be able to generate of adequate number of training positions. Similar trends are appearing also in other countries, where this situation until the end isn't settled.

Additionally in 2003 an agreement was entered into among the Ministry of National Education and Sport and the Connection of the Polish Craft (CPC, polish ZRP)). This agreement assumed the cooperation of both sides to the purpose of the improvement in the state and the quality of the vocational training, in particular in the practical organization apprenticeships. For CPC tasks among others organising of networks of businesses, in which practice will be conducted, advice was included in relation to directions of the education and fitting them to demands for the labour market, the promotion of the practical apprenticeship or supplementing the base of the practical education. However how they are showing statistics, only a 43%[54] of pupils of fundamental vocational schools in school year 2007/08 entered into an agreement for the apprenticeship with the employer. Apart from that activity aimed at the synchronization of directions of the vocational training with market requirements aren't bringing adequate results to the work what appearing is attesting to of some competition (e.g. economic assistant, seller, cook of the cafeteria) on leading places of the surplus competition for the long term. The high level of unemployment is attesting to it amongst persons about qualifications associated with some directions of the vocational training and appearing of this competition on leading places of rankings of the surplus competition. The role of enterprises in the vocational training is connected also with a conflict of interests between employers and the public sector and individual pupils. Employers will be interested in the training and practice mainly when qualifications get by pupils are enough specialist so that they can be used only in their companies. Much smaller stimuli to support the vocational education by enterprises will appear in case of the greater flexibility of employees, allowing for freer changes of the competition and employers. However a model of the more general education, reducing the risk of unemployment which can result is scenario more favorable to individual pupils from peculiar conditioning associated with the given workplace is a narrow branch of the production. Letting stimuli for ensuring bigger employing employers can assume the form of subsidies, tax breaks or the possibility of paying lower pays for training employees[55].

Apart from that with additional brake of modernizing the vocational training, of particularly a practical education, in the region of Pomerania, poor and outdated

---

[54] On the basis of data the GUS - downloaded from sides www.stat.gov.pl.

[55] Ł. Pyfel, R. Jaros, P. Krajewski, M. Wochna, *Recommendations concerning needs in the vocational education*, INSE, Warszawa 2010.

equipping school workshops and Centres of the Practical Education is (CPE) into machines, tools, devices, materials. Directors of these institutions claim that the majority of centres of the practical education is being financed in one piece by bodies of the local self - government as budgetary authorities. If this is the case pays of teachers and attendants and running costs of objects are consuming the majority of financial means, whereas the small part is allotted to investments. It means low abilities of updating the techno base - teaching of vocational training and practical. What's more, to schools a duty of refinancing for individuals for person in charges of the practical apprenticeship of the costs of purchase of working clothes and household detergents was moved. The same persons from the Pomeranian province are emphasizing that a financial base is the serious problem practical about the education - both buildings, and the machine - made equipment. The vocational training costs more than secondary school, and introducing exaggerated frugalities causes heavy losses much in effects of teaching compared with teaching the theoretical knowledge. The technical equipment very much quickly is becoming outdated, even machines and devices purchased in the period of creating first CPE (second-half of the nineties) are already most often outdated, as their technical condition is quite good (small wear and tear) and they aren't bringing the direct income, there are no financial resources for their exchange. This coming into existence of significant differences causes the rich sponsor between equipping CPE and new plants or the ones which they found. However the large, new units based on the foreign capital most often have own education systems of employees and then are avoiding the cooperation with existing institutions of the vocational training[56].

---

[56] M. Kabaj, *Program project of implementing the dual education system in Poland,* IPiSP, Warszawa 2012.

8.1.3.7. The dual system of the vocational training as the response to needs of the labour market in the Pomeranian province

One of proposals to solve day-to-day issues of the vocational education, implementing the dual system in Polish conditions is, following the example for example of German solutions. Implementing analogous system solutions we are dealing with which in the German system of the vocational education, would require the radical transformation of the system existing in Poland. Considering the possibility and the sense of implementing the dual system of the vocational training in Poland, one should clearly emphasize that the interaction between sides of the vocational education in part is being carried out. According to examinations[57] the 80% of schools and the 75% of Centres of the Practical Education from the Pomeranian province in fact are cooperating with entrepreneurs. What essential, very entrepreneurs declaring desire for such cooperation. Such cooperation takes place in general based on partner agreements signed among the school and the enterprise and includes the practical apprenticeship above all. It is also important, that pages of such agreements, are judging the cooperation very positively, as such which is bringing them mutual benefits. The cooperation initiative among the school and the enterprise in general lies on the side of a headmaster (often being based for his private contacts with entrepreneurs), however very enterprises in general are demonstrating the lack of knowledge take back the possibility and legal forms of undertaking the cooperation. In relation to above, justified delivering legal frames to the such cooperation seems to be highly, along with distinct determining her principles, what in practice would mean the implementation of the system of the dual vocational training in Poland. With second, very positive example of applying the educational answers similar to the dual system in practice, there is an undertaken cooperation

---

[57] *Examining functioning of the system of the vocational training in Poland.* Final report, Ministry of National Education, National Centre of supporting the vocational education and Constant, Warszawa 2011.

between schools and craft chambers. According to data of the Connection of the Polish Craft[58], in 2001, 157 000 pupils of vocational schools were able to undergo the practice in the enterprise. These practice was organized based on agreements of individual schools with entrepreneurs consisted in the Connection of the Polish Craft. One should here clearly underline, meaning involving the Association of the Polish Craft in enabling pupils of vocational schools to undergo practice preparing them for the real performance of work. In 2010/2011 on average 40%[59] from the 225 000 total number of pupils of vocational schools (in the Pomeranian 13 250 province of pupils) could be involved in a work practice what constitutes their 90 000 total (in the Pomeranian province of 3750 pupils). He/she is marking it, that in Poland, including in the Pomeranian province, we are dealing from unofficial functioning dual education systems what is - for the here and now - largely carried out thanks to active employing the Connection of the Polish Craft[60].

In this place one should also mention that in texts of many documents of the European Union it is possible to find suggestions concerning reforms of the structural educational systems of member states. Liberalizing the labour markets, providing to the labour market with the qualified staff, increasing the employment, and hence raising the competitiveness of economies are a general objective of proposed changes of member states, as well as the economy of the entire community. It is possible to rank among the most important documents of this type:

---

[58] Based on CPC data downloaded from the sidewww.zrp.pl/Dzia%C5%82alno%C5%9B%C4%87ZRP/Zmiany

[59] On the basis of data from M. Kabaj, *Program project of implementing the dual education system in Poland*, IPiSP, Warszawa 2012.

[60] E. Lechman, *Dual system of the vocational training in Poland - chances and barriers of the implementation* (expert opinion), Gdańsk 2012.

- Lisbon strategy (2002)[61] - which need to raise the quality of education and the rise in education expenses is pointing - new impulses for young people;
- White paper of the European Commission (2002)[62] - which puts emphasis for taking the cooperation between the educational market and the labour market;
- Recommending the European Parliament and the European Council from 23 April 2008 on establishing the European Qualifications Framework for the learning by the entire life[63] - which is being focused on the framework of the classification in the individual competition.
- Strategy Europe 2020[64] (direct continuation of guidelines of the Lisbon Strategy) - which is regarding the most important establishments in the social policy and economic in the destination of supporting the growth in the economy. To rank among the most important establishments of the document it is possible, such action which will be: they pushed the sustainable economic growth, supported the social inclusion with the special pressure on the job creation (what is a condition necessary for ensuring the height of the home-produced product). Additionally reaching the indicator of the employment is a specific objective of the strategy of persons in the century 20-64 is flying on the level of the 75% (at present it is 68%), the percentage of people prematurely giving the research up should not exceed the 10% (at present it is 13% 26), whereas what important - in assumptions - for Poland he should not exceed the 4.5%[65].

---

[61] *Lisbon strategy - road to the success of united Europe,* Office for Official Publications of the European Communities, Warszawa 2002.

[62] *New impulses for the European youth.* White paper of the European Commission, European Commission. Directorate-General for Education and Culture, Poland, Ministry of National Education and Sport, Warszawa 2002.

[63] Recommending the European Parliament and European Councils from 23 April 2008, on establishing the European Qualifications Framework for the learning by the entire life, Brussels 2008.

[64] Europe 2020, *Strategy for intelligent and of sustainable development supporting the social inclusion,* European Commission, Brussels 2010.

[65] E. Lechman, *Dual system of the vocational training in Poland - chances and barriers of the implementation* (expert opinion), Gdańsk 2012.

8.1.3.8. Declared action assumed by authorities for the development of the vocational training in the Pomeranian province[66]

1. Simple and consistent strategy of rebuilding the image of vocational schools - creating the identification/ of the identity of individual kinds of schools, promotion of the careers guidance amongst senior pupils, from the JST initiative and very schools.
2. Effective cooperation with chosen crucial employers on the local market, in contributing to educational programmes, organization of traineeships, building places of employment for graduates (e.g. patron classes of the company Toyota, inviting for the cooperation on the part of the Shipyard in Gdańsk, of Gdynia).
3. Promotions of examples of the effective cooperation on the line of the school - business (good understanding needs of employers, the flow of information).
4. Positive attitude of employees of employment offices - leading the social dialogue with employers, members of provincial advice of the employment, purpose like of best getting to know needs of the labour market.

8.1.3.9. Summary and Recommendations

It appears from gathered data and information that graduates of vocational schools more often see themselves in the role of employees than employers. Calling graduates about one's professional plans next time are most interested in getting employing the contract of employment on principles. He is a valid application is hugging graduates, that vocational schools, than aren't preparing to finding the better job and establishing an own company.

---

[66] *Studying the system of the vocational training in Poland.* Report of the quality inspection amongst experts, Ministry of National Education, Warszawa 2011.

He is an alarming signal, fact that pupils in spite of the more often declared involvement in optional classes, still on quite rock bottom under the angle preparations for the future career are assessing the educational offer.

The skeptical evaluation of the own knowledge and abilities, in it is improving the predisposition to conducting own activity low evaluation of the educational offer.

Pupils during the learning are already taking first efforts of entering the market of work. One should and so exploit their potential and enable them to take up work during the learning by developing the cooperation with entrepreneurs from the area provinces. The contact with world of the business could spur pupils into action.

One should pay attention to the fact that pupils more often seek practical experiences, than the theoretical knowledge. A substantial amount of readings is attesting to it for gaining professional experience as part of practice or the regular career.

Also a fall is watching each other, towards previous years of an interest of pupils in staying in the place of learning/settling - to convince them for staying after the school in the Pomeranian province above all the best tender of the labour market could - internships, practice and the permanent work.

Additionally the institutions responsible for the help to graduates in going the labour market up, should start acting in concert, and not shift the responsibility for the existing situation. It is regarding both very vocational schools and authorities' self-government - in it of course of public labour market institutions. One isn't allowed also to forget about the role of entrepreneurs, which apart from ceaseless complaining and the criticism of school curricula carried out by schools, should go behind the example of other EU countries - so as Netherlands or Germany, and to participate actively in the forming of the professional figure of graduates leaving walls of the school. In this way they are only able to guarantee the professional human capital for oneself in their enterprises.

The close cooperation of entrepreneurs with vocational schools will allow to predict how the labour market will look like in the future (in 5-10 years), and as a result to educate the graduate about the desired knowledge and abilities. Simultaneously the educational offer should inspire the development of specific fields of economics. Initiating establishing the partnership among vocational schools is a role of local self-governments, with entrepreneurs, because these entities are creating exactly the labour market.

Developing the strategy of educational action in the region on the professional level one should take the including education into account:
1. The economic situation - currently diagnosed.
2. The situation on the market of the work - also the one forecast.
3. Of expecting employers.
4. Demographic situation.
5. Widely understood availability of educating on every level.

Summing up, according to the authors of the study, in order to improve the quality of education practical and to bring the school closer to needs of local and regional enterprises in the Pomeranian province, it is necessary in the systematic way to implement the dual education system at vocational schools. It results above all from best examples and experience of countries the most developed of Europe which thanks to the improvement of the quality of educating by systematic implementing the dual education system are creating optimal conditions to the connection of world of educations and the business. Thanks to that for system which is creating natural coordination mechanisms of the labour market, apart from the equalization of the youth unemployment which in an optimal way is functional in the global economy, without the problem all investments in the vocational education are increasing, because three sides, i.e. self-government bodies, schools and the business are participating in this process.

Therefore, according to the authors of developing, in entire Poland, theses in it of course in the Pomeranian province, one should gradually and systematically commence introducing the system of the vocational training on the not only professional, but also average level (ultimately also higher) in the similar scope to other countries of the European Union, e.g. German.

Bearing in mind the complexity of the entire system and completely different outside and internal conditioning (macro and microeconomic), it is necessary to undergo the implementation of the system according to following stages carried out, depending on the scale, on the national level, regional or even local:

The first stage:

Purpose - elimination of formal and legal potential barriers.

Action:
- creating transparent instruments of financing the vocational education which will enable to raise funds for the modernization of the existing infrastructure;
- active policy of the state towards employers which are cooperating with schools - developing the system of incentives for enterprises;
- enabling (formal and legal) of current starting departures of the vocational training, being a response to needs of local labour markets.

Level: nationality

The second stage:

Purpose - creating the strategy of introducing the dual system of the vocational training throughout the country, but at the close cooperation with regions.

Action:
- consultation with social partners; Level: regional.
- signing the social contract which contains:

- scope of co-operation while preparing programs of the education;
- principles of financing pupils during the practical apprenticeship in enterprises;
- rules of improving teachers of professional objects;
- other ways of supporting the institutions responsible for the vocational training; Level: nationality.
– appointing the dual vocational training in regions of advisory institution responsible for coordination of activities aiming at the implementation of the system - should be in her line-up: representatives of the business, the self-government, the Labour market institution and the scientific community; Level: regional.

The third stage:

Purpose - connecting the vocational education with the economy.

Action:

– determining the long-term strategy of the vocational training in Poland, considering current trends on the labour markets including forecasts of the future - current update; Level: nationality, regional
– drawing the map of the labour market up on the microeconomic level in order to eliminate all divergences; Level: local.
– upper secondary schools must establish the cooperation with enterprises what will enable the practical apprenticeship inside them, based on the infrastructure had at its disposal by them; Level: regional (maybe local).
– creating the database available to all, where:
- schools will present the educational offer;
- employers will announce situations vacant or also traineeships;
- Labour market institutions will be presenting reports, statistical data or also forecasts; Level: regional.
– including enterprises into the current update of programs of the vocational training; Level: regional.

The fourth stage:

Purpose - popularizing innovative forms of the vocational training.

Action:

- conducting a promotional campaign directed at the local communities, being aimed at a change of perceiving the image of the vocational education. Level: regional.

8.2. Vocational education and training in Baltic Sea Region – Problems to be addressed[67]

The Baltic Sea Region is deemed the most innovative and economically strong region of Europe which has not exploited its potential yet. At the same time, however, there is the emergence of revolutionary developments which can strongly limit the economic dynamics of the Baltic Sea Region and which require an increased commitment, especially in terms of educational policy.

Such an evolution of educational policy is the key to the design of a fulfilling life and the social integration of each young person. Such improvements are also prominent in the interest of the economy which faces a completely different labor market situation.

By 2030 the number of employed persons in the Baltic States with the exception of Sweden will decrease up to 25 per cent. The quantitative problems cause a substantial intensification of qualitative constraints. The requirements of companies towards trainees are high and still increasing. Personal and social skills are equally important to the factual knowledge. In most Baltic Sea States an increasing number of graduates lack the required competences.

---

[67] Dr. Jürgen Hogeforster, Hanse-Parlament, Germany

There is a growing competition for skilled young people among SMEs, large enterprises, universities/colleges and government agencies. Moreover, small and medium-sized enterprises, which provide about 70per cent of jobs, threaten that they become losers and are pushed towards lower levels. Securing trainees with good qualifications and high level of innovation is a question of survival for SMEs in the Baltic Sea Region.

Increased immigration to the Baltic Sea Region is required; attractive educational offers are a crucial factor here. The society must open up and meet the multicultural challenges. Above all, the domestic potential should be exploited in a better way. Educational policy must ensure that the proportion of young people leaving school without qualifications as well as non-trainable adolescents is reduced significantly. No young person should be excluded, everyone deserves a second chance.

The overvaluation of purely intellectual ideals of education has to be contrasted with the eminent character of education which appeals to all sensed and encourages the acquisition of all intellectual, artistic and manual skills equally. School education always seems to lead to more uniformity. Much more individualized instruction with personal learning objectives and success is urgently needed.

Such holistic education with a promotion of individual talents is needed urgently for both weaker and stronger learners. An elite education is not sufficiently pronounced in many countries and it should no longer be a taboo. Systematic promotion of the strongest without the exclusion of the weakest is the decisive factor for the integration for all.

Early childhood education must be greatly expanded on the basis of the example of a few Baltic States. This includes sufficient number of places in kindergartens and a mandatory one-year preschool with the best and best-paid teachers.

The mere creation of new structures cannot bring any lasting improvement if they are not preceded by far-reaching cultural reforms with improvements in quality. Evolution of cultures almost inevitably leads to the growth of new structures. School structures perform a secondary role. Also a structured educational system can bring success in the case of high-level permeability. Long learning together is not a prerequisite for good school education but it facilitates teaching personal and social competences and promotes sustainable integration. The success in most Baltic States suggests that learning together should be implemented as long as practicable.

The attractiveness of vocational training has decreased very sharply in all Baltic States and in some countries it reached an alarmingly low level. The proportion of practice in vocational education must be increased significantly, especially in countries with educational systems. Vocational training should take place in the dual system.

The introduction of uniform Baltic Sea Region entrance requirements of vocational training which is determined job-specifically is desirable. Specific ways of vocational education need to be introduced with complete transparency for children with learning difficulties but also for stronger learners.

Vocational education is too separated from other branches of education and quickly leads to dead ends. A complete transparency in vocational education as well as between vocational education, general education and university education with smooth transitions and recognition possibilities is urgently needed. This includes also the Baltic-wide right to study with fellowship or specialist degree, following the example of some Baltic States.

Small and medium sized business, particularly the craft sector, must open up more strongly for employees outside the profession and to win them over to a permanent employment. Tailor made teaching phase, precise further education as well as opening of the education systems and improvement of the permeability support this process.

Young people avoid vocational training and prefer studies. However, most coursed are largely theoretical and not sufficiently focused on the practical issues of SMEs, which cannot obtain a sufficient number of entrepreneurs and skilled workers despite a large number of students. Dual courses of study which combine vocational training or activity with studies have to be established on a broad basis.

Stays abroad during training and professional activities promote increasingly important international knowledge and experience, and at the same time personal and social skills. The Baltic-wide un-bureaucratic recognition of vocational training and further training qualifications is a crucial prerequisite.

Moreover, the reduced transport and communication costs increase the mobility of production factors. Companies migrate to locations with higher potential of professionals and workers, to locations with attractive educational opportunities and diverse labor markets. The local competition for (highly) skilled workers is more intense. A uniform educational policy in the Baltic Sea Region has to be anchored in the EU Baltic Sea strategy and ensure that this competition takes place not only within the Baltic Sea Region; to the contrary, through excellent education it strengthens the competitiveness of the whole Baltic Sea Region towards other regions and expands the existing projections.

The considerable opportunities of the Baltic Sea Region can only be exploited at the highest level of innovation and excellent qualifications. Educational policy is also to a large extent connected with locational, regional and spatial planning policy. Education promotes innovations and competitiveness and includes the main support task for small and medium-sized enterprises. Educational policy must therefore be superior to all other policies and needs to enjoy highest priority also in the EU Baltic Sea Strategy. In accordance with the EU strategy "Europe 2020" politics, economy and society of the Baltic Sea Region must address their outstanding position of educational policy and recognize that the investment in human capital is the safest and the most profitable investment.

8.3. Survey on the dual system of the vocational education in Baltic Sea Region

Results of the written survey[68]

In order to obtain more detailed information related to the vocational training in the countries of the Baltic Sea Region: what are the existing problems in VET? What are the reform requirements? What are the Best Practices? ect., Hanse-Parlament carried out a written survey from June to September 2014. 11 countries took part in this survey, with most answers coming from Germany (31%) and Poland (43%).

Different institutions have participated in the survey:

38 % - chambers and other SME organizations

21 % - high schools and universities

16 % - vocational schools

12 % - other organizations

8 % - public administrations

5 % - SMEs

Two thirds of the respondents have extensive or very extensive experience in the sphere of vocational training; one third of them has very little or no experience.

---

[68] The survey was carried out by Hanse-Parlament within the project „Dual Vocational Education", part-financed by the European Union, EUSBSR Strategy for the Baltic Sea Region, Seed Money Facility in 2014.

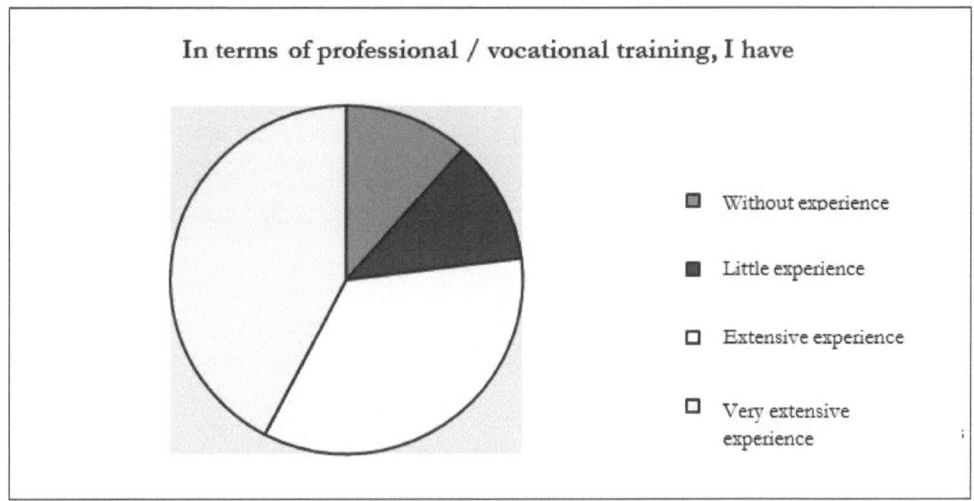

The majority of the respondents states that in their country the vocational training lasts at least 2 – 3 years and maximum 3 – 4 years. This duration of training is considered to be exactly right by more than 90 %. Noteworthy is that according to the answers in the Baltic countries the short duration of training of 1 – 2 years is mentioned comparably often and this fact is criticized by many for being too short.

In the majority of countries intermediate and final examinations are used by the chambers (70 – 80 %). The higher the share of chambers as examining institutions is, the more positively the existing examination system (more than 90 % of satisfactory answers) is evaluated.

In Germany the dual system is prevailing in the vocational training, the experience therewith is evaluated almost exclusively as very good and excellent. In the Baltic States and to a lesser extent in Poland according to the opinion of the respondents on the contrary there are first of all school systems with more or less practical training at the enterprises, whereby the part of the duration of training at the enterprise is 25 % to maximum 50 %. In these countries there is hardly any experience with dual systems; if there are any they are evaluated as "could be better". In all the participating countries it was unanimously determined that the requirements of the labor market related to vocational training can be considered in the dual system best of all.

In the German-speaking countries high youth unemployment is first of all attributed to the inadequate level of preparatory training and to the too low motivation of youth as well as to the very low level of support by the parents. In Poland and in the Baltic States the main reason for high youth unemployment is however seen in the existing corresponding system of vocational training with mainly school training and in addition to this in the level of motivation of youth which is too low. The respondents state practically unanimously that the comparably lower unemployment, for example, in Germany, Austria and the Netherlands or Denmark shall be attributed first of all to the prevailing system of the dual vocational training.

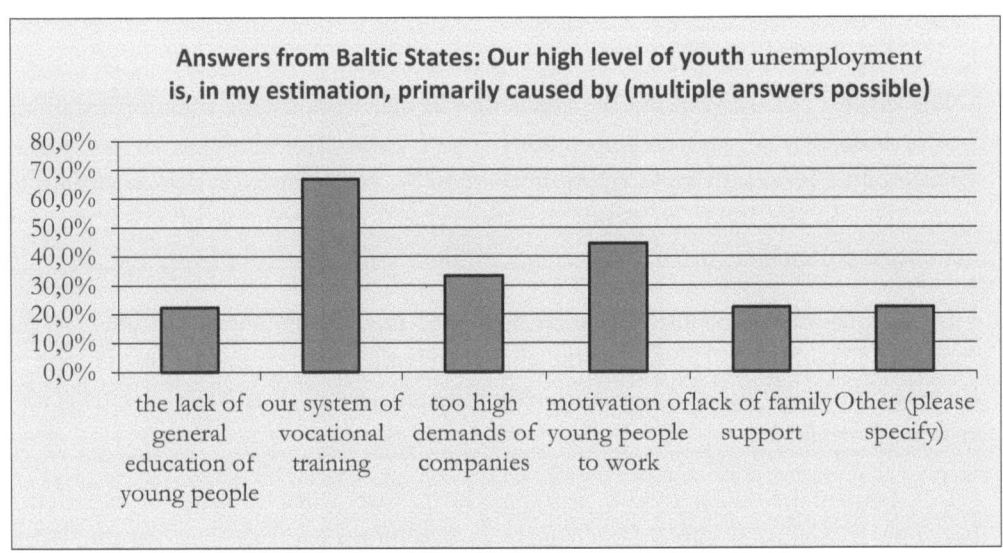

The similar situation is with the answers concerning reasons for the very low level of attractiveness of vocational training. In the German-speaking countries the main reasons are reported to be very low permeability between vocational and general (high school) education, and the feeling of getting stuck at the dead end related there-thereto and therefore also lack of promising outlooks. Concerning answers from Poland and the Baltic States, the prevailing system of school-based vocational training with insufficient transfer of skills and the concern of ending up in dead end are dominating.

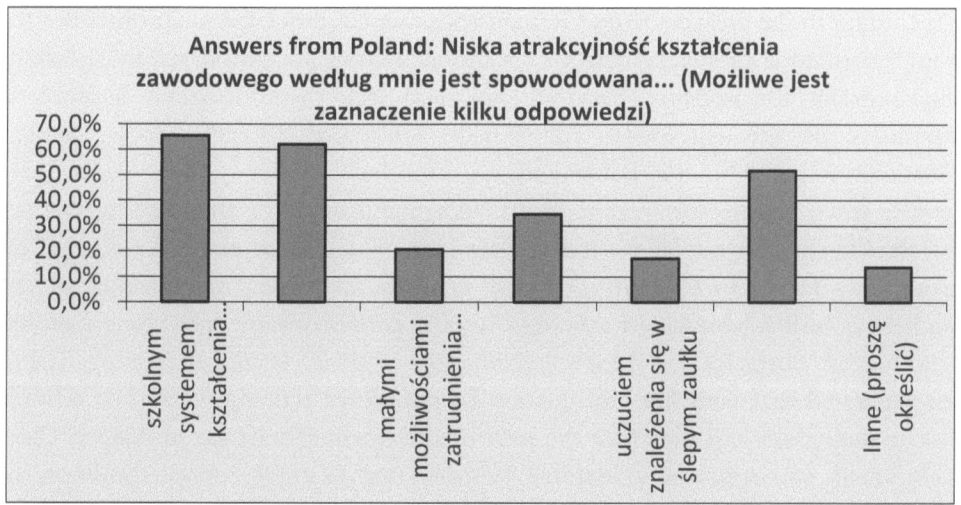

The need for political reforms in the field of vocational training is evaluated in the countries with the dual system as being low and in the countries with school-based training as being very high and urgent (up to 100 % of the answers). Firstly only in Finland there is no need for reforms: the competence-oriented vocational training has proved to be successful, the clear structuring as well as especially the full permeability between vocational and higher education and therefore avoiding dead ends should be highlighted.

On average 69 % of respondents from all the countries voted that in the dual system the training at the enterprise should be provided at the same time with the training at vocational schools on a full-time basis. The training at vocational schools in the form of blocks is considered to be of little importance. Only in Poland 26 % of respondents require that the training should first of all take place at the vocational school and only after that at the enterprise.

In almost all the participating countries (with the exception of Finland) the respondents wish that in the future the vocational training was consistently implemented in the form of the dual system. Almost without exception all the respondents stated that introduction and further development of dual systems has lots of advantages.

According to the answers from German-speaking countries the main obstacles for the implementation of dual systems of vocational training are considered to be lack of political desire for reforms, existing laws, and lack of information as well as unreadiness of the enterprises to provide vocational training places. Similar evaluations come from the Baltic and the Scandinavian States; here participants relatively often additionally regard insufficient competence of the chambers as an obstacle. On the contrary in Poland besides lack of desire for political reforms and existing laws failure to obey at vocational schools, insufficient competence of the chambers as well as absence of training places at enterprises are very often regarded as the biggest obstacles for the implementation of dual vocational training. It has been suggested that with the introduction of vocational training vocational schools will lose their tasks and therefore the jobs of the teaching staff are in danger. Clear development concepts for vocational schools, for example, upon condition of undertaking additional tasks in the field of vocational further training, are required.

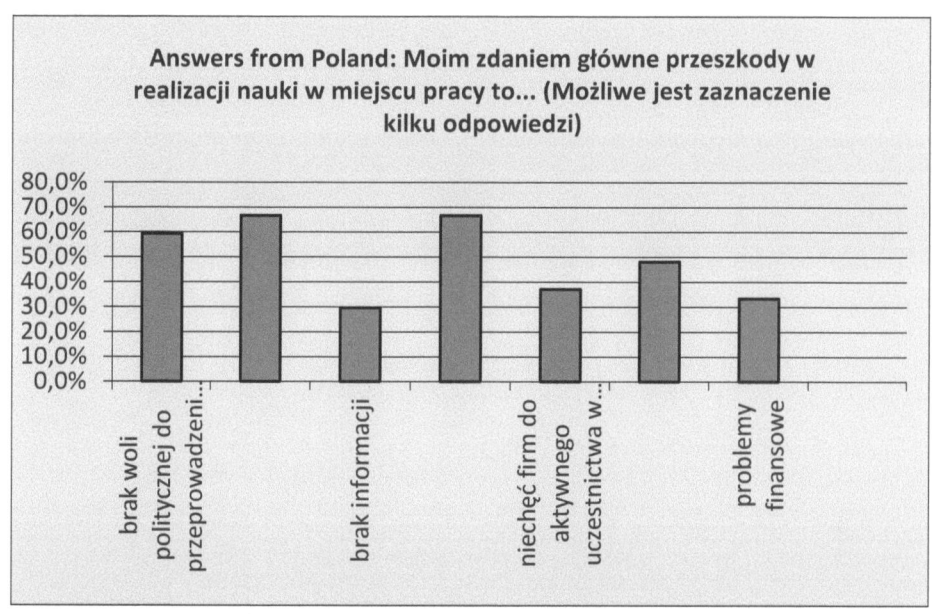

For the successful implementation of dual vocational training systems all the coun- countries regard cooperation with chambers as representatives of the enterprises as well as with vocational schools and public administrations as important, very important and essential.

On the average about 70 %, in Poland even more than 90 % of the respondents for the successful introduction and implementation of dual vocational training demand additional competences and powers of the chambers. In this regard it is considered that the chambers work close to business, they can better and more cost-effectively perform consulting and monitoring activities and therefore the sovereign powers of authorities should be granted to the chambers as economic self-government.

The respondents from all the countries have unanimously stated that high schools and universities can greatly promote the implementation of dual vocational training programs and therefore in this regard they should be engaged in a more intensive manner. In this respect the respondents mention, for example, a more intensive cooperation with employment organizations, involvement during the preparation of curricula and also sharing knowledge about new technologies. Students of vocational schools should be directly involved in research and development projects, teachers at vocational schools could visit lectures together with the students. At the same time it is determined that universities should then pay more attention to the professional life.

Summary

11 countries have participated in the survey; two thirds of the respondents are experts in the field of vocational training.

The existing deficits can be mentioned especially in the existing school-based vocational training, in small duration of training and in really excessive separation between vocational and higher education.

The dual system of vocational training is mainly evaluated very positively. Better interlocking concerning requirements of the labor market and as a consequence low level of youth unemployment are referred to as the most important advantage.

With the exception of Finland respondents mainly wish for consistent introduction and further development of dual vocational training.

The main obstacles for the implementation of dual vocational training are said to be lack of desire for political reforms, failure of vocational schools to obey and insufficient readiness of the enterprises to provide places for training at the enterprise.

For the successful dual vocational training the intensive cooperation of the actors is obligatory. A stronger engagement of high schools and universities is desirable. For the chambers mainly additional competences in the field of vocational training with the transfer of official duties to the economic self-government are required.

In the countries with mainly school-based vocational training the introduction of dual systems is of great importance and the most important approach to the reduction of unemployment, securing the demand for professional specialists and also strengthening innovations and increasing the prosperity. Corresponding projects shall

- involve various countries with different experiences concerning dual and also school-based vocational training.

- include intensive cooperation of the main actors which are vocational schools, SMEs or chambers as representatives of enterprises, high schools/universities as well as relevant public administrations.

- follow the sustainable development process and correspondingly secure international networks and also regional cooperation of the actors in the long run.

- be based on integral concepts which include, for example, information and motivation of the enterprises and vocational schools, training or trainers at the enterprise, clear development concepts for vocational schools, promotion of competences of chambers and intensive involvement of high schools/universities.

- support political reform efforts, inform about the policy and the administration through partners on an ongoing basis and during workshops and conferences it shall be directly involved in development and implementation steps.

Currently discussions about the introduction of the dual vocational education, resp. work-based learning in the existing school systems, which include this specific vocational education learning form, run over all in the Europe. One of such discussions took place in Hamburg during the Hanseatic Conference 2015. The results are presented below.

8.4. Work-Based Learning around the Mare Balticum – Results of the Working groups[69]

The Tenth international Hanseatic Conference dealt with the topic "Work-based Learning around the Mare Balticum". During the Hanseatic Conference current project results, developments, tasks and strategies are presented in short presentations and panel discussions. However, the heart of the Hanseatic Conference consists of working groups, which are internationally and interdisciplinary staffed. In more than 20 working sessions over 100 scientists, entrepreneurs and representatives from chambers, politics and administrations of all Baltic Sea Region countries developed strategic approaches to the development and promotions of vocational training and innovations for Small and Medium-sized enterprises.

Philipp Jarke, journalist, summarised the results of these working groups in painstaking work, which are presented in the next chapter.

Implementation of Work-Based Learning

How can work-based learning and particularly dual vocational training be implemented? Which way would have to be followed?

Implementing the dual system in countries that have no or little experience with it is not simple and won't work if it is forcefully implemented. **Work-based learning should be regarded as a cultural change, not only an organisational adaptation process**. The implementation of **the dual system is a process**, so that **all stakeholders need to be integrated** (integrate political and business stakeholders early on). This way the concept can be customized for the regional needs.

---

[69] Philipp Jarke, *Work-Based Learning around the Mare Balticum – Results of the Working groups* in Philipp Jarke, Max Hogeforster (eds.), Work-based Learning around Mare Balticum, Hamburg 2015, 224 – 230.

In order to shape the regional implementation process, a **committee of experts from vocational schools and companies** should be build. **Goals for both sides have to be defined**, and the committee can combine the views of both sides to develop the dual system. In order to make the change happen, **supervisors, competence and willingness** are needed.

As in the work-based learning programmes a relevant part of the training is taking place in the companies, it cannot be completely controlled by central institutions, unlike in vocational school. In order to make sure that all apprentices learn all skills and gain all knowledge necessary for their profession, **standards have to be developed (determine the quality of work-based learning; a definition of dual vocational training has to be found)** and basic **regulations have to be implemented** (also important: **identify regulations that hinder the implementation of work-based learning**).

In order to make dual vocational training a success, the school side of the system must not be neglected. The schools also need to be reformed as e.g. **work-based learning is not taking place in centres of practical training**, and some **teachers resist to cooperation with companies**. But the **vocational schools** also have to **be promoted**. For example in some areas of the BSR there is a **lack of vocational school teachers**.

Changing a system is always difficult. It needs a change in **regulations, funding (finance)** for the institutions and **PR** to change employers' opinion. **Addressing the companies that could potentially train young adults** is key to success: Without the support of the companies the dual system will never work. Therefor **we should discuss not only the disadvantages for the companies but stress the advantages (stress the benefits for both sides)**.

To raise the awareness of the possibilities of the dual system, **work-based learning should be promoted by showing examples of regionally well-known people's careers. The importance of knowledge AND practical skills needs to be emphasized.**

Clusters should be created where stakeholders of all parties develop the system. Before that can happen, **reliable data is needed**, and **surveys about which skills and qualifications are needed**.

Are there obstacles to the implementation of work-based learning?

The implementation of work-based learning knows many obstacles, simply because in many BSR countries it means a change to the well-known system. And change most of the time feels unpleasant.

Companies or **business** in general may **not** be **interested** in taking part in vocational training as they regard education and training of young adult as a task that public bodies have to take care of. They may **lack** fundamental **understanding** of the chances of training the apprentices themselves, that they can teach them the exact skills needed in their particular company, that they can identify the most talented young adults in real work environments instead by studying CVs and test results, etc.

To be fair, training young adults on the jobs means additional costs for the company, at least in the beginning when most supervision is needed. Therefore the **companies do not want to employ the students without additional funding (lack of governmental funding)**.

Some companies also lack trust in their apprentices or students. **They** may **regard students as potential competitors**. Therefore they are not willing to share their knowledge and experience with them.

But the mind-set and knowledge of the young adults sometimes also is an obstacle to work-based learning. The **motivation of young adults** to take up a vocational training position is low in some BSR regions, and the **level of basic education** is problematically low among parts of the youth.

The educational system in general is to be changed in many parts of the BSR in order to implement work-based learning effectively. **Rules and laws** have to be passed and the **information exchange between the relevant institutions has to be improved** in order to support this goal.

Is there demographic management in SMEs? Will it be used as a strategic tool?

SMEs have difficulties in finding new skilled employees; therefore **seniors have to be kept in companies because of their experience and their relations to customers.**

But the **companies** also **need new** and younger **employees.** The **young generation has different skills (e.g. ICT).**

In general a lack of demographic management was found in most SMEs of the BSR (**no demographic management in SMEs; there is no demographic management of SMEs in Russia, Belarus and Ukraine**).

Lithuania is regarded as an exception to this rule: **In Lithuania employing and supporting seniors, young adults and females are used as a strategic tool as well as the creation of healthy work environments and the circulation of good experiences.**

Differentiation in Vocational Training

Is there a need for differentiated ways of vocational training for slow learners, "normal" and strong young learners?

There was an overwhelming majority of participants who wish that the vocational training system should offer differentiated paths for young adults as their knowledge and skills acquired in school is covering a wide range from poor to exceptionally good. **In order to have more educational variations and options the education systems have to become more flexible.** E.g. if an **apprentice finds himself in the wrong profession, he should be allowed to change to another profession, taking into account his previously acquired skills and knowledge.** Vocational schools should **try to include these** students **in normal classes.**

Ideally, the **curricula of vocational training courses should be customised individually according the potential of the individual student** (although some voices stated that **the share of applied/practical training within different voca-vocational training schemes should be the same** and that **there should be a fundamental agreement about how may days or hours per week the apprentices are learning on the job in the enterprise instead of in school**).

As apprentices are very diverse, **the basic curriculum in vocational schools needs to be changed**, and **diverse vocational training paths should be establish in educational systems**. Especially for the least talented and the most talented young adults the traditional vocational training system does not offer the best choices.

For example **in Germany, for many young adults the requirements of vocational training positions are too difficult to meet**. Lots of young adults drop out of school, they lack basic skills like calculating, spelling, punctuality and reliability. It is very hard to make up these deficits after the young adults have finished school. Instead, **the school system has to integrate the employers' (practical) requirements into the curricula**.

For the future, the **weak learners need individual tutoring from public school until they have reached first stage of vocational training**. Such **preparation for vocational training raises the chance to get a vocational training position later on (e.g. in Poland)**.

The weaker students' deficits often cover theoretical knowledge rather than practical skills. The companies have to **identify diverse practical tasks for young adults with diverse levels of talents** and **create jobs/professions for weaker learners**. The **companies** also **have to improve the educational and pedagogical skills** of their staff, so that they can support their weaker apprentices better. But with practical skills only, these young adults nowadays cannot get a degree. Therefore **differentiation of vocational training options is needed for young adults with learning difficulties**. These young adult have to be supported; **smaller classes for weaker students/apprentices** are one possible way to do this. **Weaker students also should be offered additional lessons and individual support by teachers and mentors**. By this means, more of the weaker learners should be able to meet the basic requirements of the vocational training programmes. But some may still not be able to graduate e.g. as a craft journeyman, as the formal and theoretical requirements are still too high. For these **weaker learners the education systems lacks a quali-qualification degree below the degree of the craft journeyman**.

But also for the very good learners, they system has to be made more attractive: **Additional training- and study programmes for e.g. high school graduates have to be implemented**, so that SMEs have got better chances to attract and employ these young talents. **More dual study programmes**, combining academic studies with vocational training, are needed. This would **raise the attractiveness of SMEs for most talented young adults**. But these **dual study programmes should not only implemented in prestigious professions** (e.g. also in the **building sector**).

Implementation of Dual Study Programmes

What are the advantages and disadvantages of dual degree programmes? How about the sustainability for SMEs?

Advantages

There seem to be a lot more advantages than disadvantages of dual degree study programmes. In general, dual degree study programmes contain **less theory and more practice** than traditional study courses. And due to their **practice**/practical experience in the companies in **real working conditions**, the students have got an **understanding of the topic** they are studying theoretically.

There are close feedback circles between the university/college and the companies. Accordingly, the **latest requirements of the enterprises regarding qualifications are being taken into account** and integrated into the curriculum. This makes the **usability of qualifications for both, the students and the enterprises**, unique.

As the students are working in the companies with colleagues and customers, they **learn interpersonal and social skills** which would not necessarily be the case in a traditional study programme. The same goes for **experience in the use the use of tools and technology**. Due to their close contact to other workers in the company **they speak the same language as shop floor staff** which makes it much easier to build bridges between blue and white collar staff. The graduates combine the advantages of both, vocational trained employees and university graduates: They **know practices (VET) and can supervise (BSc) because they have knowledge in project management and leadership**.

All of these advantages **prepare the students for the job better** and make it **easier for the graduates to find a job**. If they prefer to set up their own business, they also benefit from their dual study programme (**students learn about setting up a business and about knowledge transfer**).

For **SMEs** dual degree study programmes are a means to **recruit talented apprentices** and **to keep best apprentices in the enterprise**, respectively. One could say: **Dual programmes are made for SMEs**.

Disadvantages

Dual study programme are not made for everybody, as **the workload is very high** compared to traditional study programmes. Another problem for students is the **lack of financial resources**. Traditional funding institutions that support students with grants and scholarships do not cover dual degree programmes. This puts an additional financial burden on the students who often have to pay fees for their courses.

Dual degree students are very much focused on the requirements of the company they work in (**concentrated at one enterprise**); therefore their flexibility is reducing (**less flexibility**). There are **strong (sometimes restricting) ties between student and employer** – but the students have best chances to get hired after graduation.

How is the implementation of dual degree programmes possible? Who should do what? Which goals and measures would you propose for implementation?

Introducing dual degree study programmes in countries that do not even have dual vocational training programmes could be difficult (**transfer in Baltic Sea Region not until dual vocational training has been established?**). The educational system should be transformed one step after the other. Another option is to start pilot programmes to test the viability (**pilots needed**). These programmes need **financial support by the member states (enterprises and state programmes)**.

In some BSR countries little is known about the requirements of the industry: **What does the industry think about dual study programmes** are an important question to be answered. Surveys have to be conducted.

But nevertheless in the long-run **harmonisation of legislation and qualifications is needed in the BSR. An EU-funded project is needed to start this process.**

Within each country the **legislative framework** has to be change by **the government**, dual study degrees have to be accredited and fully acknowledged. **The ministries have to implement the necessary measures**, and to fasten up this process, the **ministries have to cooperate better (cooperation between ministry of economics and ministry of education)**.

The **educational institutions have to change the basic training programmes**, and the teaching staff has to be prepared for their new tasks: **There is a lack of vocational teachers holding master's certificates.**

Within the companies a change of the way of thinking has to take pace also: **The way of thinking of the members of staff has to change. Dual degree study programmes need staff motivation**, as the workload will increase for the working students.

If the implementation of dual degree study programmes proofs to be a financial burden for the companies, **resources for compensation** are needed. Otherwise only few enterprises will take part in the system.

8.5. Strategic Programme of the Baltic Sea Academy - Promotion of Dual Systems of Vocational Education

Background

The Hanse-Parlament – an association of 50 chambers of commerce from all the Baltic Sea Region states – and the Baltic Sea Academy – an association of 17 colleges/universities from 9 Baltic Sea Region states – conduct the project "Future perspective: One-year Professional Qualification (Hamburg Model)" within the Life Long Learning Programme in cooperation with chambers, universities and other educational institutions. The model of one-year vocational education in the dual system had been developed and successfully implemented in Hamburg for young people with special support needs. It integrates these young people better into the vocational education, makes their career choice more secure, lowers the drop-out rates and significantly increases the chances on the labour market. The one-year vocational qualification can be recognised as the first year of vocational education, when thereafter the vocational education can be continued in the regular dual system.

In framework of this project, the Hamburg Model is transferred to Lithuania and Hungary, adapted to region and country specific conditions and implemented in these both countries. In addition, the possibilities of future implementations are examined extensively in Latvia, Norway and Poland. All the project results will be transferred to all members of the Hanse-Parlament and the Baltic Sea Academy. These chambers of commerce, industry and crafts and colleges/universities promote the future implementation of dual vocational training in general and the Hamburg Model specifically. The present strategic programme pursues the dissemination of the dual systems of vocational training in as many regions and countries of the Baltic Sea Region as possible.

Assignment of Tasks

Vocational education has lost much of its attractiveness over the last years. Especially in the so called new EU Member States (e.g. Poland, Lithuania, Latvia and Estonia) with predominantly school-based vocational education, the participation in the vocational education is low; it has even dropped to an alarmingly low level, and is perceived by many young people as a dead end. In some countries e.g. Lithuania one or two-year courses are often conducted within the school-based vocational training, which open to young people a faster entry to the labour market with higher earning potential but by no means qualify them sufficiently and rather increase youth unemployment. There are usually only short internships in enterprises, so that work-based learning is very limited. The result is the unemployment of 15 – 24-year-olds in Lithuania, Latvia and Poland at the level of 28 – 30%. Insufficient professional qualification leads to long-term unemployment of youth, which for example for people with only primary and lower secondary education, is at the level of 20% in Poland, 28% in Latvia, and 40% in Lithuania.

In some countries, up to 15 % of school leavers cannot start vocational training, have to wait in long queues or receive no professional training at all and are quickly bound to be unemployed. Up to 30% of young people, who begin vocational education, break it completely or change the profession.

At the same time, enterprises complain about the lack of skills of graduates. Vocational training at schools can meet only limited needs of the labour market and takes into account the qualification requirements of enterprises inadequately. The students do not learn the daily routine at a working environment sufficiently and the increasingly important personal and social skills can be taught in the classroom in a very limited way. According to a survey conducted by the Baltic Sea Academy in enterprises in Lithuania 70% of the SMEs need additional professionals whom they can attract in a very limited way or cannot attract at all. 96% of the SMEs want a better practical training and 74% a better theoretical training.

As a result of demographic changes, the number of school leavers in all the Baltic Sea Region states is decreasing, with the exception of Sweden. By 2030, the number of employees at the age of 15 – 44 will decrease by up to 25%. In most countries there already exists a shortage of skilled workers, which will have a more significant impact in the future, and will strikingly limit the developments. At the same time, we can observe alarmingly high youth unemployment, especially due to the lack/shortage of professional qualification.

SMEs threaten to become losers in the competition for qualified young staff. Due to a lack of qualified employees, innovation level is already much lower than it actually might and should be. The lack of young entrepreneurs, managers and professionals limits the growth of the SMEs the most. The improvement of qualifications with the simultaneous removal of the shortage of skilled workers are the most important support tasks and the key to sustainably strengthen the innovations, competitiveness and growth in SMEs in the Baltic Sea Region.

Given this, it is of vital importance to emphasise

a) the integration of young people and reduction of youth unemployment as well as

b) the provision of qualified employees for SMEs and a significant reduction of the shortage of skilled workers in generally.

The German system of dual vocational training, which leads to a comparatively low youth unemployment, integrates enterprises responsibly in the provision of junior staff as well as connects vocational education much better with the requirements of the labour market, can make very large contributions with a lasting impact to the achievement of objectives. However, the German system cannot be misunderstood as a "patent model", which must be simply transferred. An adaptation to the respective regional/national conditions is always mandatory. Nevertheless, the basic principles of the dual model should be maintained to the greatest possible extent; "work-based learning" that consists of more or less short periods of internship in enterprises is by no means sufficient. Therefore, the present strategic programme by colleges and universities includes high-level objectives in as many regions and countries of the Baltic Sea Region as possible:

a) to sustainably promote the implementation of the adapted systems of dual vocational education as well as dual bachelor's degree programmes, which combine professional education or work with studies.

b) to sustainably support the implementation of the adapted Hamburg Model with a greatly improved integration of young people in vocational education as well as reduce youth unemployment.

c) to provide qualified staff and thus also promote innovation and competitiveness in SMEs.

8.5.1. Action Programme "Hamburg Model"

Hamburg Institute for Vocational Education in Hamburg developed this professional qualification and has been using it for the last five years. It is a proven method to integrate young people into professional education, who cannot find vocational training opportunity. While or after one year of learning the students can continue with regular dual professional education.

The training begins with classes at the respective vocational school for few weeks. Then, the participating students pass different company and school based learning phases. The young people receive intensive advising, learn about enterprises and different professions, choose a professional training and get the corresponding training opportunity.

The "entry phase" in vocational training by the Hamburg Model is provided up to one year, after that the young people continue their regular education in the chosen profession. The first year can be credited to the entire training period. The teaching and learning contents match those of the first year of training in the dual system of vocational education.

The involved colleges and universities (see section 6.1) sustainably promote the future implementations of the Hamburg Model for the better integration and vocational education of young people, and the introduction of dual bachelor's vocational training (see section 3.) in their respective regions and countries. The folfollowing activities are planned for this purpose:

- Joint consultations, regular exchange of information as well as mutual sharing of experience in the context of member meetings and working meetings of the Baltic Sea Academy.
- As a part of the respective daily business, provision of information and documentation concerning the Hamburg Model to different target groups, for example public administrations, employment services, vocational schools, politicians, etc.
- Participation in third-party events as well as undertaking own workshops and conferences to present and discuss the Hamburg Model.
- Transfer of the Hamburg Model as well as the specific concepts and evaluation results of the initial implementations within each activity and area of dissemination.
- Specific concepts for the implementation of the Hamburg Model had already been developed for Lithuania and Hungary. Implementations are tested and the implementation plans are prepared for the countries of Latvia, Norway and Poland. These concepts are used for information and transfer purposes and create an important basis for the participation of colleges/universities in the adaptation of the Hamburg Model to the respective regional/national conditions of different countries.
- Process consulting and assistance with the implementation of the Hamburg Model.
- If necessary, carrying out evaluations of implementations of the Hamburg model.
- Demand-oriented implementation of training of vocational education teachers, consultants and instructors as well as the training staff of participating companies.

In the course of the work process and the experience gained, it is possible to develop and implement further measures to promote the implementation of the Hamburg Model.

8.5.2. Action Programme "Dual Vocational Education and Dual Studies"

Colleges/universities are supposed to be involved in the most important activities for the implementation of dual educational systems, since they have the necessary scientific capacity, lay the essential foundations in teaching and research, can take over development and adaptation tasks and are ideally suited for the relevant information and advisory tasks. Therefore, colleges/universities should develop a Baltic Sea Region-wide network of promoters, consultants and supporters to assist the implementations and thus together with chambers of crafts, industry and commerce and other public institutions to strengthen the chances of success and sustainable introduction of dual vocational studies in Baltic Sea Region.

The 17 colleges/universities of the Baltic Sea Academy have already received the following detailed documentation:

- Analyses of labour and education markets in Baltic Sea Region
- The dual system of vocational training in Germany
- Concepts and curricula for dual bachelor studies

These and other relevant concepts were discussed together during workshops and international conferences. On this basis, colleges/universities sustainably promote and support the general implementation of dual vocational training and dual degree programmes in the Baltic Sea Region states. In this ways, colleges/universities will be gained to be promoters of dual vocational education and will give assistance implementing dual vocational trainings. In this context, the following activities are planned for the time being:

- Joint consultations, regular exchange of information and experiences at the members' and working meetings of the Baltic Sea Academy.
- As a part of the respective daily business, provision of information and documentation of the dual system of vocational education for various target groups, such as enterprises, training institutions, politicians, public administrations, etc.

- Participation in third-party events as well as undertaking own workshops in order to present and consult the dual system of vocational education.
- International conferences and the Hanseatic Conferences with politicians, employees of administrations, representatives of companies and educational institutions to present and discuss dual education systems and possible implementations.
- Transfer of the German system of vocational education as well as best practice examples from different countries (e.g. Denmark and Norway) in the respective activity and dissemination area.
- Provision of information and advice to politicians, administrations, vocational schools, enterprises, etc.
- A particular shortage situation in countries with predominantly school-based vocational training results from the fact that experienced and qualified staff is rarely available at enterprises. In order to remove these bottlenecks, it will be necessary to introduce the following measures:

a) "Training for trainers in companies" with completion of a trainer – aptitude test will be integrated in study courses, so that the junior entrepreneurs already receive the necessary qualifications.

b) Implementation of trainings "Training for trainers in Enterprises" in order to prepare the enterprises optimally for the implementation of dual vocational training courses.

c) Implementation of "Training for trainers in enterprises" in chambers and other educational institutions, so that the personnel in enterprises could be trained on a broad basis.

- In the case of dual training, about 2/3 of the total training time is spent in enterprises. Thus, it has a natural consequence that in the case of a transition from school-based to dual vocational education in vocational schools, the personnel and space capacities will be released. The fear of losing a job is a major limiting factor for appropriate reforms. Offering further education, for that there is a great need but limited offerings in the Baltic Sea Region, can be one of the new fields of activity of professional schools, to keep human resources. Baltic Sea Academy and Hanse-Parlament both had already devel- developed around a dozen further training programs and successfully tested in practice in different Baltic Sea Region countries. The present concepts and curricula are transferred to vocational schools, implemented there and Train-the-Trainer seminars for vocational school conducted.

- Implementation of further training for vocational teachers, coaches and advisors.
- Provision of dual systems of vocational education within the framework of study offers for teachers at vocational schools.
- Support in the adaptation of the existing system of dual vocational education in the relevant regional/national conditions.
- Process consulting and assistance with the implementation of dual vocational training.
- Intensive exchange of experience and wide dissemination of information about the requirements, concepts and possibilities concerning dual degree programmes.
- Individual members of the Baltic Sea Academy are already implementing seven different dual bachelor's degree programmes. The existing concepts, curricula, experiences, etc. are transferred and individual implementations are tested.

All the members' and working meetings of the Baltic Sea Academy include joint consultations, feedback, further development of the existing educational and promotional measures as well as the development of new ones. Further relevant promotion projects, which are exemplified in the following section, are implemented to cope with these extensive tasks.

Implementation and Realisation

The ongoing implementations of the aforementioned activities are coordinated by the Baltic Sea Academy within the framework of its day-to-day business. In addition, Hanse-Parlament informs all its members (see section 5.2) fully, involves them according to their demand and organises co-operations between colleges/universities and the chambers of commerce, industry and crafts in the respective regions.

The Baltic Sea Academy ensures at the same time consultations, regular exchange of information and transfer of experience. As a result of the consultations, further development of the existing measures and the development of additional measures is decided upon and determined who will conduct these works under the lead of the Baltic Sea Academy.

The regular exchange of information and experience as well as manageable works will be financed from own resources of both institutions and their members. Complex work and development tasks should be implemented within the framework of the existing or new funding projects.

For the implementation of more elaborate events, more complex development tasks as well as for the implementation of the educational measures, further projects will be developed within EU or national funding programs, which will then be applied for and implemented by numerous colleges/universities or in cooperation with the Baltic Sea Academy.

On the basis of the past experience and the present results, it has already been decided that during the project "Hamburg Model" by September 2015, under the lead of the Baltic Sea Academy and the Hanse-Parlament, several major projects will be developed and applied for, in particular:

- Growth of Green Jobs in Construction Branches – Increasing Employment in Energy SMEs
- Dual Vocational Training for the Qualification and Integration of Young People and the Strengthening of Innovation in SMEs
- Sectors Skills Alliance 'Management and Technologies of Water, Waste Water, Waste and Cradle to Cradle"
- Closing the Skills Gap, Tuning Graduates' Qualifications to Labour Markets' Needs

- Establishment of a Baltic Sea Region-wide Education and Competence Centre "Energy Efficiency, Climate and Environmental Protection, Including Resource-efficient Construction"

Vote

The present strategic programme was developed, discussed and agreed within the project "Future Perspective: One-year Vocational Qualification (Hamburg Model)" by the project partner Baltic Sea Academy, all other project partners and the involved universities and colleges. The members of the Baltic Sea Academy were involved as associated partners and during their members' meeting on January 20, 2015 they discussed the programme and decided to implement it in the future.

Other Publications by the Baltic Sea Academy

Volume 1

Strategies for the Development of Crafts and SMEs in the Baltic Sea Region

2011; ISBN: 9783842326125

Volume 2

Strategy Programme for education policies in the Baltic Sea Region

2012 (2nd edition); ISBN: 9783848252534

Volume 3

Education Policy Strategies today and tomorrow around the "Mare Balticum"

2011; IBSN: 9783842374218

Volume 4

Energy Efficiency and Climate Protection around the "Mare Balticum"

2011; ISBN: 9783844800982

Volume 5

SME relevant sectors in the BSR: Personnel organisation, Energy and Construction

2012; ISBN: 9783848202577

Volume 6

Strategies and Promotion of Innovation in Regional Policies around the Mare Balticum

2012; IBSN 9783848218295

Volume 7

Strategy Programme for innovation in regional policies in the Baltic Sea Region
2012; ISBN: 9783848230471

Volume 8

Humanity - Innovative economic development through human growth by Kenneth Daun
2012; ISBN: 9783848253395

Volume 9

Economic Perspectives, Qualification and Labour Market Integration of Women in the Baltic Sea Region
2013; ISBN: 9783732243952

Volume 10

Corporate Social Responsibility and Women's Entrepreneurship around the Mare Balticum
2013; ISBN: 9783732278459

Volume 11

Development of the enterprises' competitiveness in the context of demographic challenges
2013; ISBN: 973732293971

Volume 12

Age, Gender and Innovation – Strategy program and action plans for the Baltic Sea Region
2014; ISBN: 9783735784919

Volume 13

Innovative SMEs by Gender and Age around the Mare Balticum
2014; ISBN: 9783735791191

Volume 14

Innovation in SMEs, previous projects in the Baltic Sea Region and future needs
2014; ISBN: 9783735791191

Volume 15

Building the socially responsible employment policy in the Baltic Sea Region
2014; ISBN: 9783735790484

Volume 16

Women and elderly on the BSR labour market - good practices' analysis and transfer
2014; ISBN: 9783735791412

Volume 17

Manual and Best Practices for Innovative SMEs by Gender and Age in the Baltic Sea Region
2014; ISBN: 9783735791405

Volume 18

Civilizational changes and the competitiveness of modern enterprises

2014; ISBN: 9783732282449

Volume 19

Female Entrepreneurship – Evidence from Germany and the Baltic Sea Region and analysis of women`s activity in SMEs in Poland

2014; ISBN: 9783735757296

Volume 20

Manual for trainings and dual study courses of the sector skills alliance "Skills Energy BSR"

2015; ISBN: 9783734750120

Volume 21

Work-based Learning around the Mare Balticum

2015; ISBN: 9783734776151

Volume 22

The Hamburg Model – exemplary integration of youth into vocational education

2015; ISBN: 9783738630060

Members of the Hanse Parlament

The Chamber of Craftsmanship and Enterprise in Bialystok

Brest Department of the Belarusian Chamber of Commerce and Industry

Hungarian Association of Craftsmen Corporations

Cottbus Chamber of Skilled Crafts and SME's

Dresden Chamber of Skilled Crafts and Small Businesses

Pomeranian Chamber of Handicrafts for SME's

Hamburg Chamber of Skilled Crafts and Small Businesses

Kaliningrad Chamber of Commerce and Industry

Chamber of Craft Region Kaliningrad

Chamber of Crafts and SME in Katowice

Chamber of Crafts and SME in Kielce

Handicraft Chamber of Ukraine

Handicraft Chamber Leningrad Region

The Craft Chamber of Lódz

Belarusian Chamber of Commerce and Industry

Minsk Department of the Belarussian Chamber of Commerce and Industry

Mogilev Branch of Belarusian Chamber of Commerce and Industry

Russian Chamber of Crafts

Warmia and Mazury Chamber of Crafts and Small Business in Olsztyn

Chamber of Crafts in Opole

Master of Crafts Norway

Eastern Mecklenburg-Western Pomerania Chamber of Handicraft

Panevezys Chamber of Commerce, Industry and Crafts

Wielkopolska Craft Chamber in Poznan

Latvian Chamber of Crafts

Craft Chamber in Rzeszów

Schwerin Chamber of Skilled Crafts

The Chamber of Handicraft Middle Pomerania in Slupsk

The St. Petersburg Crafts Chamber

The Chamber of Crafts and SME in Szczecin

The Baltic Institute of Finland

The Organisation of Handicraft Businesses in Trondheim

Vilnius Chamber of Commerce, Industry and Crafts

Small Business Chamber Warsaw

The Lower Silesian Chamber of Craft and Small and Medium-sized Businesses

Kyiv Chamber of Commerce and Industry

IBC Innovationsfabrikken Kolding

Donskaya Craft Chamber in Rostov/Don

Nordic Forum of Crafts

Members of the Baltic Sea Academy

Brest State Technical University, Belarus

University 21 non-profit limited Liability Company, Germany

Hamburg University of Corporate Education, Germany

Hamburg Institute of International Economics, Germany

Hanse Parlament e.V., Germany

International Business Academy, Denmark

Lund University, Sweden

Satakunta University of Applied Sciences, Finland

University of Latvia, Latvia

Gdansk University of Technology, Poland

Panevezys College, Lithuania

Hanseatic Academy of Management, Slupsk, Poland

Saint-Petersburg State University of Economics, Russia

Tampere University of Technology, Finland

Vilnius Gediminas Technical University, Lithuania

Vilnius Pedagogical University, Lithuania

University of Bialystok, Poland

Võru County Vacational Training Centre, Estonia